My Secret Rome

A Girl's Guide to Intimate Rome

Original title: *My Secret Rome*
2014 © L'Airone

Translation from the Italian: Sandra Tokunaga

Cover and graphic design: Germana Giorno
Cover illustrations: Alice Del Giudice

Photo credits:
© Domitilla Petriaggi
Fotolia: © anna Filitova, © giampaoloS, © laguna35,
© Pavel Klimenko, © Giuseppe Parisi, © GialloZafferano,
© Rawpixel, © lassedesignen, © umiberry, © berc, © Subbotina Anna,
© Gian Paolo Tarantini, © pogonici, © bellopropello, © Sandor Kacso,
© Kzenon, © Marzia Giacobbe, © fusolino, © Vitos, © Porechenskaya,
© Kaponia Aliaksei, © Kesu, © Sergii Figurnyi, © sborisov, © jovannig,
© MasterLu, © Beboy, © orsinico
Stock.xchng: © kate709, © tellgraf, © cissaborba, © nhasan, © chewjoel, © eyebiz
Vector Open Stock: © artshare
© Alice Del Giudice

Printed and bound by: Conti Tipocolor – Calenzano (FI)

2014 © Gremese
New Books s.r.l. – Rome
www.gremese.com

ISBN 978-88-7301-771-4

Manola Costanzi
Domitilla Petriaggi

My
Secret
Rome

A Girl's Guide to Intimate Rome

GREMESE

Preface

The book you are about to discover should be read as if it were a delicious and original recipe. Its main ingredients call for the beauty of Rome and your own personality and curiosity. It should be savored, therefore, as a whole. Let yourself surrender to even the most unexpected and original flavors of this recipe. If you would like to recreate it, always remember to add a pinch of your own personality to everything you do. This will give a unique flavor to your experience, and your recipe for visiting and enjoying the Eternal City will be truly special and inimitable. Our idea was to rework the ancient flavors of Roman tradition, rekindle the Capital on the flame of modernity, then ice it with a chic and trendy touch. After that, it will be up to you to express it all in your own personal style!

GLAMOUR

My Secret Rome Recipe*

Ingredients
Fantasy: 1 bottle
Fashion addiction: As needed
Curiosity: 200 g
Social Life: 70 g
Fun: As much as you like
Creativity: 150 g
Naughtiness: A pinch

Method
Sift 200 grams of curiosity and eliminate any lumps of conformism and monotony.
Uncork a bottle of fantasy to dissolve your curiosity until you are daring enough to be ready for any new adventure.
Add 70 grams of V.I.P. social life until you are uninhibited enough to create a sensation at any important event in the Capital.
Take 150 grams of creativity and blend with all of the above until you can find a solution to almost anything the city has in store for you.
Sprinkle with enough fashion addiction to know that those shoes you absolutely adore will be terribly in fashion next year.
Add a pinch of naughtiness, always for a little zing, to enjoy all the fun this book can bring.

* In this recipe, as in all the other recipes that you will find further on, the quantities indicated use Italian units of measurement. Always remember that:
100 grams (g) = 3.5 oz.
100 milliliters (ml) = 3.4 fl. oz.

Strokes of genius... luck
... and lightning

Use this calendar to note the date, place and maybe even who you were with when:

You managed to pass a test without studying:

Bought the fabulous T-shirt that all the girls copied:

Talked your way out of a huge fine:

Grabbed the last pair of those shoes you couldn't live without, and at half price:

Received an SMS from someone you thought had disappeared from your life:

Went to the beach on a cloudy day that turned out to be beautifully sunny:

Caught someone's eye as you waited at a traffic light:

Arrived right on time even though you left half an hour late:

Got a compliment from a boy who normally would have never given you a second glance:

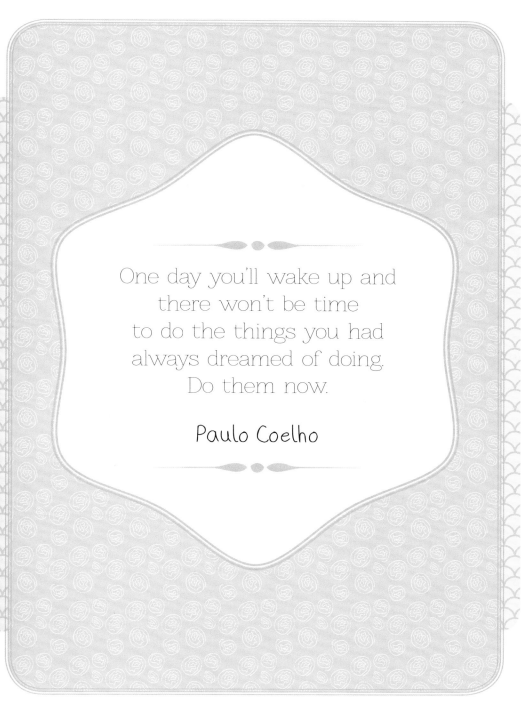

One day you'll wake up and
there won't be time
to do the things you had
always dreamed of doing.
Do them now.

Paulo Coelho

Index by subject

Contents

Dine on a roof terrace in Rome's historical center, with the "ponentino"

Who says that Paris rooftops are the most beautiful and romantic in the world? Who says that French chefs are better than the Italians? Try admiring the rooftops of Rome from the terrace of chef Riccardo Di Giacinto's restaurant **0°-300° Cold and Grill**, (Michelin one star), and this may change your ideas. Rome *caput mundi*! The chance to enjoy a stupendous view over the rooftops of Rome's historical center is not always an easy or accessible privilege, but **0°-300° Cold and Grill**, at the panoramic roof garden of The First Luxury Art Hotel, is truly unique with its breathless 360° sweeping panorama of the heart of the Capital. The master of the house is chef Riccardo himself, a renowned name among Roman gourmets for his venerable restaurant **All'oro** (located on the lobby level of the same hotel). The terrace is a sublime experience during the sizzling summer. The secret is to arrive at aperitif time, when the evening sea breeze ("ponentino") just begins to cool off the blazing Roman day. You might want to sip a flute of bubbly, or try one of barman Patrizio Boschetto's fabulous cocktails. After admiring Rome in all its splendor – linger over the sights of the Pincio, the Altare della Patria, the "Palazzaccio", the Casina Valadier, the charming terraces of the attic apartments of Rome's center – continue the evening with a dinner of tasty delights. An enchanting and spellbinding mixture of emotions and sensations.

Have fun tasting the beautiful selection of different types of bread, served with real old-fashioned tomato sauce just like all Italian

grandmothers used to make, and choose from a menu of light and appetizing specialties. Discover the extraordinary *Panzanella* (a traditional specialty from central Italy), the fresh *Misticanza*, or the tasty *Catalana di tonno rosso*, perfect for a summer dinner. From "0°", if you love *crudités*, to the "300°" of meat dishes baked in a wood-burning oven, at Riccardo's you will find everything your heart desires in an explosion of gourmet pleasures.

Yet the truly unique experience this restaurant offers, one that you will cherish as a very special memory, is the restaurant's roof-terrace dinner.

Have an intimate dinner at the highest point of Rome's center, with an extraordinary menu created by Riccardo himself. You will draw upon all of the experience of a chef who developed and refined his talent working alongside the famous Ferran Adrià. During the pauses between one course and the next (7 in all!) you will be gently cuddled by Rome's light west breeze, the "ponentino", as you gaze over Rome's rooftops for an evening to remember for the rest of your life!

Hurry, though, before everyone else, so that you can be the first to tell them about your fantastic discovery!

0°-300° COLD AND GRILL – ALL'ORO RESTAURANT
Via del Vantaggio, 14
Tel. +39 06 97996907 / +39 393 9448268
info@ristorantealloro.it

Open Monday through Sunday from 7:30 pm to 11:00 pm
Food Cocktail Bar: Monday through Sunday from 6:00 pm
to half past midnight
Reservations: booking@ristorantealloro.it

Watch a short film in a cinema created by Louis Vuitton

Once upon a time there was the Cinema Etoile (Rome's first cinema), where for decades people lined up to see films such as *Roman Holiday*, *Rome Open City*, *Bitter Rice* or *La Dolce Vita*; a place whose name alone evokes the history of Italian cinema and all of the magical atmospheres bound to it. The French fashion house Louis Vuitton has always nurtured a sensitive interest in the seventh art. A few years ago, it decided to infuse new life into this historic space so loved by the Romans. Yet it also wanted to preserve its original nature.

The eclectic architect Peter Marino spent several years working for Louis Vuitton on a plan to restore the space. The concept was to transform the location into a cultural boutique.

The historical suitcases and trunks that have always been a symbol of the famous fashion house serve as supporting pillars for a structure on three levels where art exhibitions, short films, high fashion shows and a bookshop all boldly mix.

As you step through the door you are immediately struck by an impressive elliptical staircase that ascends in great curves. Light and transparent, it is immersed in a warm luminescence that softly pervades the environment. The encounter of the prestigious Vuitton hides and jewelry with the magic of cinema (a film screen in a large open theatre forms an integral part of the shop) inspires us to dream. As we ascend

the great staircase or linger to admire the fabulous constellation of Vuitton creations, we easily become a famous diva of the silver screen or a dazzling star on the stage of an opera house.

Poised between dream and reality, take a seat in the little cinema on the first floor (with its 18 big armchairs and lovely little bookshop surrounded by Vuitton creations) and treat yourself to some recent short films or to one of the classic masterpieces that built the legend of Rome's oldest and most beloved cinema of all time. To make it all the more legendary, the screen is placed on the very spot that it occupied in the historic Cinema Etoile.

Don't miss the chance of visiting what has to be the most unique boutique in the world: amidst famous scenes with Sophia Loren or the fascinating gaze of Marcello Mastroianni, you might even let yourself be tempted by an accessory or two that are so popular these days. Ready? All right, "Action!" Let's buy!

LOUIS VUITTON ROMA ETOILE
Piazza di San Lorenzo in Lucina, 41
Tel. +39 06 68809520

Have a beauty treatment in the vault of a bank

What do the *Divine Comedy* and a bank vault have in common? The answer is simple: a beautiful spa in the center of Rome in the fascinating **Aleph Hotel**.

Adam D. Tihany, a famous American interior designer, drew inspiration from Dante's *Divine Comedy* to create the interior decoration of the Aleph, a hotel that is part of the Boscolo chain.

Indeed, the decoration of the hotel is based on the ingenious idea of contrasting Dante's Inferno and Paradise: below is Paradise, represented by the Spa (and its soft colors, such as cream and blue), and above, the Inferno, represented by the communal areas and restaurant (in more striking colors, such as red and black).

Aleph's Spa is original and intriguing, set in a bank vault, which was what it was before becoming a hotel. An impressive, curious steel-clad door (the original vault door) leads to the seductive Spa immersed in every shade of blue.

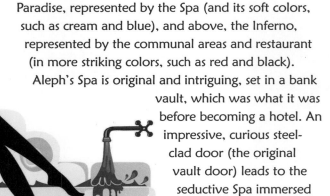

You plunge into an atmosphere that evokes all of the indolence of the ancient Romans as they cared for their bodies, enveloped in sensuous and refined rituals in the sauna, Turkish bath and two pools.

The luxury you enjoy in this fascinating space is typical of a five-star hotel. So, be prepared to let yourself be pampered by extraordinary treatments and massages for a truly unique experience.

And, if you really want to go all out, you can even reserve the entire Spa to organize a highly original private party, or a naughty farewell to spinsterhood, which will definitely be anything but banal. Whatever event you create, you can rest assured that whatever happens in the vault will definitely remain in the vault! There's no safer place!

BOSCOLO ALEPH ROMA
Via di San Basilio, 15
Tel. + 39 06 422901

Become a model
for a day

Leafing through a fashion magazine and admiring the marvelous photos always makes us dream. No use denying it, all of us have dreamed of being a model for a talented photographer at least once. Perhaps not everyone realizes that many of the locations used for fashion photo sets are right in Rome. So, why not take advantage of it?

The city will provide the sets, with its impressive monuments, historic piazzas, little streets lined with flowers, fountains with sparkling plays of water, panoramic views and picturesque corners. Trent photographer **Federico Nardelli** will take care of the rest. Federico, in addition to being a real professional and wonderful person, speaks fluent English and Spanish. He will know just how to immortalize your lovely stay in Rome, whether by accompanying you along your own itinerary, or by suggesting magnificent places in the Eternal City himself. In any case, he will know just how to highlight the best of your personality!

Return home with beautiful photos of you in splendid form. Allow yourself to move about freely without being weighed down by a camera. Enjoy every moment to its fullest, without having to stop and wait for the right moment. You can say that you have been a model for a real fashion photographer! You and Rome, together for a day, together for always.

FEDERICO NARDELLI – WALDENPHOTO STUDIO
Tel. +39 0461 1724437 / +39 349 8707578
info@waldenphotostudio.com
www.federiconardelli.it

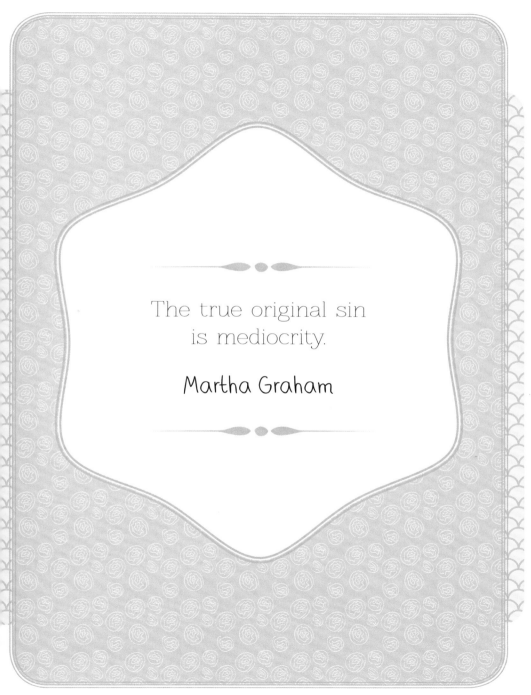

The true original sin
is mediocrity.

Martha Graham

Have a Queen's *millefeuille*

If you ask any Roman what the best pastry shop in Rome is, he will certainly point you to the one in his neighborhood just around the corner from where he lives.

It has been scientifically proven that for a Roman, there is nothing like the cakes that he has had since he was a child. This will consequently trigger long debates between supporters of opposing factions and schools of thought. Nevertheless, there is only one pastry shop that is famous for its unforgettable *millefeuilles*. And there is a curious city legend surrounding it.

We are talking about the **Pasticceria Cavalletti**, which has been

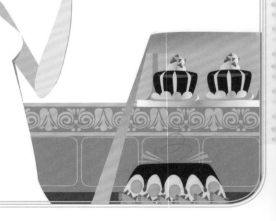

sweetening up the days of the inhabitants of the Trieste neighborhood and beyond since 1951.

Cavalletti's fame rests on its *millefeuilles*. They are made of a marvelously fragrant puff pastry (which is perfectly circular), with layers of whipped cream lightly flavored with Marsala according to, obviously, a very secret recipe. The entire pastry is covered with powdered sugar, with dashes of crushed hazelnuts on the sides. Legend has it, in fact, that even today, Queen Elizabeth II of England herself, known for her weakness for sweets, simply cannot do without them and has this mythical sweet delivered weekly to Buckingham Palace.

Whether the legend is true or not is not really our concern here. But what is certain is that you can go to this ancient Roman pastry shop to see for yourself whether its *millefeuille* is indeed worthy of a real queen!

PASTICCERIA CAVALLETTI
Via Nemorense, 179/181
Tel. +39 06 86324814

Admire Rome from a crystal lift

Want to see Rome from above, in all its splendor, but don't have the time or money to rent a helicopter?
Take the panoramic lifts up to the terrace of the **Quadrighe del Vittoriano**: in a few seconds and many fewer Euros you will be at the top of the imposing Altare della Patria that overlooks Piazza Venezia. This is the highest point of the Complesso del Vittoriano, one of the greatest works built in Rome during the nineteenth century. The monument celebrates the greatness of Rome as Italy's capital, and represents both the "Unity" of Italy and the "Liberty" of its citizens. "Patriae Unitati e Civium Libertati" are, indeed, the words engraved on the two imposing bronze quadrigas (one of "Unity", the other of "Liberty") atop the edifice. These are works created by two different sculptors, Fontana and Bartolini.
From there, you will find a magnificent view unfolding before you: the Coliseum, the Fori Imperiali, Piazza Venezia, the churches of the historical center, the Tiber, the Jewish Ghetto, the Piazza del Campidoglio and the Torre Campanaria. You will be able to see as far as the Palazzo della Civiltà in EUR, the Palazzo di Giustizia, Via Nazionale, and right to the Alban Hills.

The crystal lifts were inaugurated in 2007 and were designed by the architect Paolo Rocchi. They are built according to a semi-cylindrical structure that stands a little away from the rest of the monument. It is made of steel and crystal to give the construction lightness and also to let visitors make the most of their ascent over the city.

To take the lifts, go to the Terrazza Mediana floor, which is located on the Colonnato level. A ride of 35 seconds covers an altitude of 40 meters and will bring you to a breathtaking panorama that you definitely will not want to miss!

VITTORIANO PANORAMIC LIFTS

Entrances at:
Ara Coeli – Ala Brasini
Piazza del Campidoglio (Convento Ara Coeli)

Summer opening hours:
Monday to Thursday 9:30 am to 7:30 pm
Friday and Saturday 9:30 am to 11:30 pm
Sunday 9:30 am to 8:30 pm

Winter opening hours
Monday to Thursday 9:30 am to 6:30 pm
Friday to Sunday 9:30 am to 7:30 pm

N.B. No admittance after 45 minutes before closing time!

Do your make-up at a traffic light

To be a true Roman girl, you will have to develop certain skills and abilities that characterize the female population of this city. One of them is definitely the ability to put your make-up on while waiting at a traffic light, just to save precious minutes and arrive on time for your date or appointment.

Consider that a traffic light stays red for at least 90 seconds, and that during any normal route a girl might take she will come across at least six or seven lights. Unless she has an unlikely stroke of luck, every traffic light will change at least one and a half times. Just doing a rapid calculation, she will be forced to stop for a minimum of nine minutes to a maximum of fifteen. What an eternity! How many things you can do in fifteen minutes! It is definitely enough time to do a complete make-up job. All you need is to have everything at hand and a little practice.

What's needed:
- ✔ foundation;
- ✔ wet refresh tissues;
- ✔ eyeshadow pencil;
- ✔ mascara;
- ✔ blush;
- ✔ eyeliner (optional):
- ✔ lipstick or gloss.

It is essential to apply your day cream to your face before you go out. Then, once in the car, your make-up base is ready. At the first traffic light, apply small quantities of foundation directly on the face: forehead, both cheeks, chin, nose... and there! Estimated time: five seconds, that is, one for each spot. You will then have all the time you need to spread the foundation uniformly over the entire face to make it beautifully luminous. When you've finished this part of the operation, wipe your hands with a refresher tissue. Then you can head off to the next traffic light to perfect the work.

The more traffic lights you come across along your way, the more successful your make-up will be!

LITTLE TIP: If you're afraid that you are going to meet the man of your dreams before your make-up is finished, always have a big pair of sunglasses on hand just in case: they'll hide the "work in progress"!

Order the sexiest cocktails in the Capital

You're in one of the most beautiful capitals in the world, and swept away by the magic of Rome, you might not even remember your own name, let alone know what drink to order! With all of the many cultural and artistic stimuli, the new or old friendships, the budding romances or steadfast loves… it's normal to be overwhelmed. So, just in case your mind boggles, be prepared with a few names of cocktails bursting with personality and character, which you must absolutely learn by heart.

ROSSINI

3/10 strawberry puree
A few drops of lemon juice
A few drops of sugar syrup
Ice (as much as you like)
7/10 sparkling wine or champagne

The strawberries are beaten with a few drops of sugar syrup and lemon. After adding the ice, sparkling wine or champagne is then poured over the mixture.

This refined and chic cocktail was created in the mid-twentieth century in honor of Gioacchino Rossini, the world-famous Italian *Il Barbiere di Siviglia* composer. Referred to as the "Napoleon of a musical era" by Giuseppe Mazzini, Rossini was also famous for his unbridled passion for good cuisine and wine. He was quite a respectable enologist and an expert on wine-making. Legend relates that as a child, Rossini wanted to be an altar boy so that he might have access to the precious nectar in the Holy Mass ampullae! The cocktail named after him reflects much of the artist's playful spirit. Sipping this intense rosé colored elixir will help to add romantic and refined accents to your evening.

SEXY PASSIONATE:
MARTINI ROYALE ROSATO

1/2 rosé martini
1/2 prosecco sparkling wine (or as a substitute for prosecco 1/2 soda which will make it a "Martini Frizz Rosato")
1 slice orange
Lots of ice

Red, like the color of love and passion. Spicy and fruity, with strong accents of clove, cinnamon and nutmeg that blend with light raspberry and lemon flavorings.

And remember, once you've had this cocktail, be sure that a stitch of your knitted dress doesn't get caught on the seat of your chair, as in the 1993 commercial with Charlize Theron... there might not be the MARTINI label to cover your B Side on time!

SEXY IRONIC:
MOJITO ROYALE

1 teaspoon sugar
15 ml fresh lime juice
1 stem fresh mint
Ice (as much as you like)
60 ml sparkling water
60 ml Havana Club Añejo 7 Años
60 ml Mumm Cordon Rouge champagne

The sugar, lime juice and mint are crushed together and then diluted with sparkling water. The ice, Havana Club Añejo 7 Años, and champagne are then added.

This is the perfect cocktail for those who have a fun holiday outlook, those who appreciate freshness and simplicity and who like improvising evenings rather than having too many set plans or schedules.

In any case, whatever cocktail you choose, whether you want to experiment with something new or prefer to stick to a classic Bloody Mary, we would suggest that you plunge into the languorous and sinuous Sunday atmosphere created by the affable Marcos in the lovely garden-square **Lounge Bar** at the Hotel Locarno, just off Piazza del

Popolo. The Liberty decor of this warm and refined "guest house" (inaugurated in 1925 by the then Swiss owners with posters by the great commercial artist Anselmo Ballester), the big fireplace, the piano in the tea room and the bar near the entrance will plunge you into the Roaring Twenties. The little tables and intimate settees in the garden-square outside, pervaded by the fragrance of wisteria, will make you feel almost as if you were entertaining at home with some Roman friends and a few interesting foreigners you've just met.

HOTEL LOCARNO – LOUNGE BAR
Via della Penna, 22
Tel. +39 06 3610841 / +39 392 9100560
info@hotellocarno.com

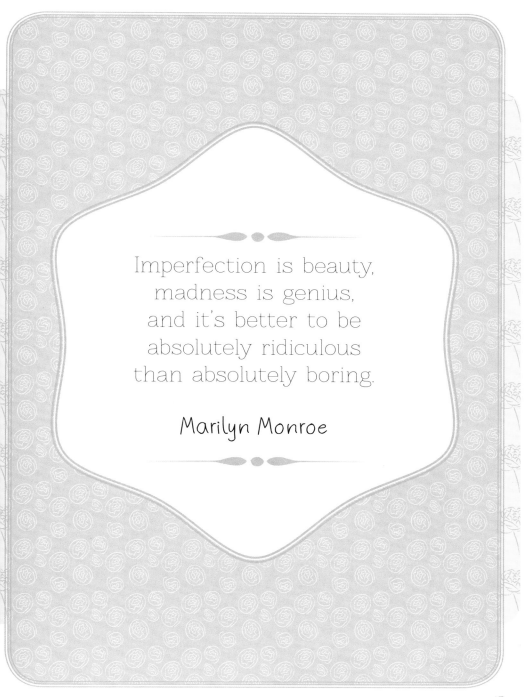

Imperfection is beauty,
madness is genius,
and it's better to be
absolutely ridiculous
than absolutely boring.

Marilyn Monroe

Dine at the same table as Madonna

How many girls, as they leaf through a celebrity gossip magazine, can recognize the restaurant where pop star Madonna had dinner? All of the most glamorous and trendy girls know exactly where it is.

Located in the heart of Parioli, the restaurant **Molto Italiano** often hosts celebrities, whether they be international stars or famous Italian names. It is not unusual to see football champions such as Cristiano Ronaldo or Francesco Totti, or famous actors there, savoring the Italian dishes of this restaurant, where traditional cuisine mixes perfectly with the restaurant's covertly international atmosphere.

In addition to the great traditional Roman dishes such as *pasta cacio e pepe*, *amatriciana* and *carbonara*, splendidly prepared by the skilful chef (Paolo Castrignano), the Molto offers excellent products and specialties such as *mozzarella di bufala*, delivered right from Battipaglia, Zibello *culatello*, and cured meats that you will rarely find elsewhere such as the Calabrian *'nduja*. Even if you're a fashion model who is always watching her figure, or a delicate gourmet who tries dishes as if she were a *Masterchef* judge, you will always feel at home at Molto Italiano, where there is always something to fit your fancy. So, put on that favorite dress of your top ten and those vertiginous heels, and be prepared for an evening of delicious glamour.

When you arrive, you will take a seat in one of the big armchairs at reception until a waiter accompanies you and your guests to your table. If it's summer, ask to sit at the table that is slightly on its own, towards the back of the terrace, on the right. If it's free, you can boast that you had dinner at the same table as... Madonna!

MOLTO ITALIANO
Viale dei Parioli, 122
Tel. +39 06 8082900
www.moltoitaliano.it – info@moltoitaliano.it

MOLTO LIBRERIA CON CUCINA
Viale dei due Macelli, 59D
Tel. +39 06 69784868

Find that rare piece to decorate your home

Between Via Giulia and Via dei Banchi Vecchi, you will find a little road where a veritable pearl of interior decoration, art and design is located.

You will immediately be struck by its quiet atmosphere and complete harmony as you linger over handcrafted objects, vintage pieces and contemporary design.

You will discover creations by Valerie Boy, the French artist so gifted in metalwork, or Tel Aviv designer Arik Ben Simhon, British designer Andrew Martin, Roman artist Nicola Guerraz, or Brazilian Ricardo Moro, as well as so many other creators.

There will be spectacular pieces produced by Lange Production, created by Serge Mouille. He is the designer of those fifties lamps that are impossible to find anywhere, and which are currently being reproduced by the Mouille Foundation.

Two floors of understated and bohemian elegance where luxury has a completely relative value, as it is inextricably linked to the personality and sensitivity of the person who experiences it.

The **SFERAotto** showroom is a treasure of contrasting concepts and products that are the fruit of refined, sophisticated and intelligent creation. It offers limited editions and unique pieces to its clientele that enhance the daily lives of those who possess them.

Coming home will be a new experience. Leave the chaos, stress and demanding challenges outside, and be regenerated in a design environment that truly reflects who you are.

SFERAOTTO
Art and Interior Design
Via delle Carceri, 5/6/7
Tel. +39 06 68892630
info@sferaotto.com

Discover the fashion labels of Roman girls

Girls from Rome have their own special style. They have their secret shops where they find the trendiest new creations, those indispensable accessories, and everything needed to create the perfect outfit for every occasion.

A true Roman "fashion victim" would never think of attending the most exclusive aperitif without that little dress that makes everyone else die of envy, or the beautiful accessory with that touch of originality that makes her special.

When you're at the most fashionable places of the Capital, you might often think to yourself, "I wonder where that little blonde – who came in greeting everyone and who was not even asked to give her name – bought those shoes or that T-shirt?" The answer: the boutique **Niki Nika**, which boasts four shops in Rome, one in Porto Cervo and one in Milano Marittima.

You'll want to spend hours browsing among all the colorful clothes, sparkling jewelry and glamorous handbags. You will surely find that article or accessory that gives you just that little extra touch of personality for a refined and indisputably trendy air.

Inspiration will come even to the most indecisive of girls or those at a loss for ideas. They have no choice but to surrender to the irresistible fashion atmosphere of these stores. If your objective is to find the perfect outfit, you'll be able to say: mission accomplished.

NIKI NIKA ROMA CENTER
Via del Leoncino, 15
Tel. +39 06 68134783

NIKI NIKA ROMA CENTRO
Via Borgognona, 4
Tel. +39 06 67982579

NIKI NIKA ROMA PONTE MILVIO
Via Riano, 5
Tel. +39 06 33221505

NIKI NIKA EUR
Viale Città d'Europa, 845
Tel. +39 06 52279428

Take a sip of Roman history

Rome has always had strong links water, and it is not surprising that the city was founded along the banks of the Tiber. Romulus was the first to realize the importance of this element. The ancient Romans took it from there and developed as many as eleven mammoth aqueducts, and they were only the main ones. These great masterpieces of architecture and hydraulic engineering made Rome famous for its beautiful fountains.

The Rome of the Caesars boasted no less than four hundred pools, and though London and Paris drank water from the Thames and the Seine, the Romans acquired the luxury of drinking source mineral water. Even today, twenty centuries later, the Trevi Fountain, the fountains on Piazza Navona, Piazza Colonna, the Barcaccia on Piazza di Spagna, and the district of Campo Marzio are all fed by the Vergine aqueduct (19 B.C.).

Rome has never known periods of drought. The network carries water not only to the various fountains, but also to the **Nasoni**. These are characteristic little cylindrical fountains, often in cast iron, and have a tap that looks like a big nose. Romans consider Nasoni an invaluable tradition. They offer free drinking water – the same that is distributed to all homes – and represent one of the many exclusive merits of Rome, the only city in the world whose fountains have been designed with the sole purpose of quenching the thirst of the population.

Most of the Nasoni have only one tap, but there also some rare ones that have more. For example, in front of the Pantheon, near its great fountain, there is a Nasoni with two taps and on Via della Cordonata, near Via Nazionale, there is one with three. There are 2500 Nasoni in Rome. We usually don't notice them, but they are a true godsend, especially in the summer!

There is a smartphone app ("I Nasoni di Roma") with a downloadable map of all the public fountains in Rome!

And since water is the most precious treasure...

Happy hunting!

Create a duckface calendar

Duckface is a purposely ironic and exaggerated expression that pokes fun at the sensuous divas of the red carpet, who often greet the public with expressions that are not the most spontaneous or natural.

Making these faces sometimes helps overcome the awkwardness of having our picture taken. Just think of Ben Stiller in *Zoolander* or Jim Carrey with his great faces. You make the expression of a duck by puckering up and pushing your lips out as far as you can, as if you were Donald or Daffy Duck.

Rome will provide a great outdoor set for an entire calendar of these poses!

Here are some suggestions for locations:

JANUARY: Piazza Navona during the Epiphany festival – as long as you get the traditional "Befana" witch to play along too!

FEBRUARY: On the Ponte di Via degli Annibaldi, the Coliseum will be your backdrop. Since it's Carnival, maybe you can ask one of the Roman centurions to participate!

MARCH: In front of the Piper, the historic club on Via Tagliamento.

APRIL: The Spanish Steps with its traditional show of beautiful azaleas.

MAY: Saint Peter's, from the Ponte Umberto I to the crossing with Lungotevere di Tor di Nona.

JUNE: Gianicolo terrace.

JULY: Trevi Fountain, just as Anita Ekberg in Federico Fellini's *La dolce vita*... but a word of warning... no bathing in the fountain, unless you want a huge fine!

AUGUST: Isola Tiberina from the Ponte Garibaldi, which links Trastevere with Largo di Torre Argentina.

SEPTEMBER: Castel Sant'Angelo terrace.

OCTOBER: Inside the Pantheon, with the big hole at the top of the dome as your background. Legend says that rain will not fall inside the Pantheon because of what is called the "chimney effect" created by the warm rising air from hundreds of candles that break up the drops of water.

NOVEMBER: Want to be "alternative"? Go to the Ponte dell'Industria (also known as Ponte di Ferro) with the Gazometro as a backdrop.

DECEMBER: Since we all become children again at Christmas, why not make a duckface at the Disney Store on Via del Corso, perhaps with Daffy Duck even?

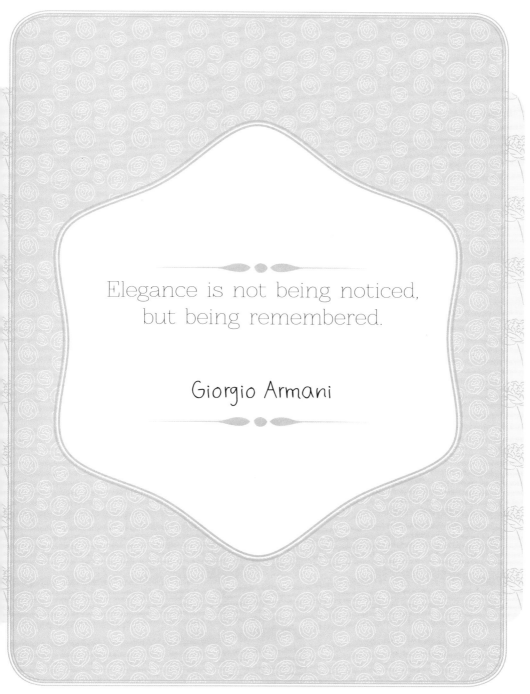

Elegance is not being noticed,
but being remembered.

Giorgio Armani

Know what things not to say on your first date with a Roman boy

Every city has its habits, every city has its traditions and the inhabitants of Rome are no exception to the rule, particularly when it comes to the male sex. There is an unwritten code, a series of rules that all girls should know to avoid making a bad impression or being guilty of some irreparable error on their first date with a true Roman.

Here are a few of these golden rules:

• Never risk expressing any pros or cons about the Capital's two football teams. You risk losing points in a snap: his favorite team is like "la Mamma" – off limits!

• Never take up the challenge of cooking a traditional Roman dish for him (*carbonara*, *cacio e pepe*, *rigatoni con la pajata*). Indeed, the way his grandmother, aunt, or mother make it (they've been Romans for at least seven generations) is unbeatable!

• Never correct any expressions in dialect or typical Roman pronunciation. Every Roman is proud of his accent. Even the most cultivated and refined young men like to show off from time to time with a colorful expression or heavy Roman intonation, just to be loyal to their "Roman-ness".

• Never compare Rome to any other city in the world. Rome is unique, absolutely beautiful and to be loved – and that's that!

• Never comment on the way he drives. The traffic in Rome is like a jungle, it's a matter of survival!

• Never force him to go shopping on a bright sunny weekend. He will want to go to the beach more than anything else in the world.

• Never tell him how late he is: in Rome everyone allows a leeway of at least ten to fifteen minutes for appointments, it's just a question of flexibility.

• Never show that you don't understand references to films considered classics (*Il Marchese del Grillo*, *Febbre da cavallo*, *Vacanze di Natale*, *Un sacco bello*...). Better to bluff your way with a nod rather than show you're ignorant on the subject. It's understandable that you might not remember the current Prime Minister's name, but not knowing Alberto Sordi's most famous line is unforgivable!

Enjoy a hammam on the ruins of Nero's baths

Spa, which in Latin is *Salus per aquam*, means caring for health through the virtues of water. In ancient Rome, baths were places to meet, communicate, relax, and above all to recuperate.

Today, psychological and physical well-being is also associated with spatial dimensions. The aim of architecture is to be a useful tool for relaxation, whether this be visual or environmental.

The Giammetta twins, students of the great Massimiliano Fuksas, are among the most avant-garde professionals of the Capital. They are the designers of the **Acanto Day Spa**, a wellness centre located just seconds from the Pantheon.

Here, architecture has a communicative function. The division of the space, the materials used, the chromatic effects and the atmosphere of the Spa are all intended to reawaken and stimulate visitors in a multi-sensorial approach. Guests need only surrender to this enchanting experience in contemporary architecture.

No detail has been overlooked. As you enter, the first area is totally white. The walls follow convex and concave curves, rather than angles. You are immediately plunged into a state of amniotic suspension, the ideal way to unwind and leave behind all the stress that has been building up.

Oxidized iron represents the work of man. The walls of opaque glass become increasingly transparent and evoke the limpidity of water and, metaphorically, the path to purification of the body and spirit.

Here, culture becomes one with well-being. Contemporary elements fuse in suggestive harmony with the vestiges of Antiquity.

The Spa is built upon the ruins of Nero's Baths and the foundations of an ancient Roman house. Rare details of this history are still present today, just as the philosophy of respecting and caring for the body has remained unchanged since these origins.

The Spa, in addition to its traditional treatments and hammam, offers various types of massage (aromatherapy, ayurveda...), as well as energy stimulating processes related to the four elements (air, water, fire and earth) and techniques for purification that draw inspiration from millenary rites.

You will feel reborn again!

ACANTO DAY SPA
Piazza Rondanini, 30
Tel. +39 06 68136602 / +39 06 68300664
info@acantospa.it

Be a princess
for a day

What girl, deep in her heart, hasn't dreamed of being a princess, even just for a day? Perhaps not every girl dares to admit it, but the truth is that the princess myth has a place in the hearts of almost every woman. Imperial or Baroque Rome might not seem the likely settings for such a dream. Perhaps England or the Loire Valley in France come to mind more readily. Yet Rome is full of surprises, even for its own inhabitants. For example, not everyone knows that they can visit the **Castello di Torcrescenza**, which is only about a ten minutes' drive from the city center. The marquis Francesco Crescenzi built this castle on the site that once played host to a tower dating back to 1100 A.D.

During the Middle Ages, the ruling family, seeking a strategic vantage point over the land, enlarged the castle. Its façade is flanked today by two impressive towers with ghibelline battlements. To access the first courtyard, you cross the moat, where a drawbridge once stood. In this courtyard, you will find two splendid fountains representing the two Roman rivers, the Tiber and the Aniene. An arch leads to a cloister with a lovely vaulted fourteenth-century portico. During the twentieth century, an iron and glass structure was constructed over the cloister to create a winter garden that is a delight to visit in any season.

Many artists have painted the castle over the centuries and others have

drawn inspiration from its landscapes. In recent decades, the castle has hosted prestigious private events and celebrity weddings of couples such as Briatore-Gregoraci and Totti-Blasi.

Entering these enchanted walls would make any woman dream. The drive up to the castle alone creates a fairytale atmosphere that is far from the chaos and frenzy of the city. The Castello di Torcrescenza is truly the perfect setting for the most beautiful wedding or memorable party of your dreams. It is a castle that would make any woman feel like a princess, if only for a day, even by simply being a guest.

CASTELLO DI TORCRESCENZA
Via Casale della Crescenza, 1
Via Due Ponti, 100
Tel.+39 334 1298125
www.castellotorcrescenza.com

Learn a few recipes
of Roman cuisine

Rich, hearty and tasty, Roman cuisine is definitely not for those who are forever on a diet. But breaking the rules once in a while is good for all of us! When you return home, why not take Rome with you by preparing a typical Roman meal for your friends? You'll be a sensation!

SPAGHETTI ALLA CARBONARA

(for 6 people)
600 g spaghetti, 3 eggs, 200 g *pancetta*/bacon,
50 g grated parmesan, pepper, 1 onion, 30 g butter,
1/2 glass dry white wine

Thinly slice the onion, dice the *pancetta*, and brown these in a pan
with butter. Add the white wine and let it evaporate slowly.
Beat the eggs in a large bowl (as if you were making an omelet), then
add parmesan and pepper. When the pasta is cooked (be sure not to
salt the water too much!), drain, and toss in the bowl with the eggs.
Add the onion and pancetta and stir. Serve hot.

SALTIMBOCCA

(for 6 people)
600 g sliced veal, 50 g *prosciutto crudo*, fresh sage,
salt, pepper, 50 g butter

Lay the slices of veal on a cutting board. They should be thin and
not too large. Put a slice of *prosciutto crudo* and a whole fresh sage
leaf on each slice of veal, then attach together with toothpicks. Heat
approximately 50 g of butter in a pan. When the butter is hot, cook
the saltimbocca on a high flame, adding pepper and a pinch of salt
(not too much since the *prosciutto* is already salty). When the meat
is browned on one side, turn it over to brown the other. When the
pieces of saltimbocca are cooked, arrange on a serving plate with
the *prosciutto* and sage leaf side up.

For a vegetable side dish, treat your guests to a surprise, drawing
upon the double culinary tradition of Rome: Roman and Jewish.

CARCIOFI ALLA GIUDIA

(for 6 people)
12 artichokes, lemon juice, salt, pepper, oil for frying

Pluck off the first leaves of the artichokes and leave the stems about the width of three fingers high. With a sharp knife, prune the artichokes of any inedible parts from the base towards the tip. Soak the artichokes in water and lemon juice (which keeps them from blackening). Drain and dry, then crush them slightly so that the leaves open like a flower. Salt and pepper the inside. Deep fry the artichokes in hot oil, with the stems up. After a few minutes, roll the artichokes in the oil to cook the stems. Once these are browned, place the artichoke stems upright again and press the artichokes delicately against the bottom of the pan. After approximately 10 to 15 minutes, once golden brown, remove the artichokes from the oil and let them rest a few moments. Sprinkle very lightly with cold water, then plunge them in the hot oil again for about 1 to 2 minutes. Drain and serve immediately!

FIORI DI ZUCCA FRITTI

(for 4 people)
8 pumpkin flowers with their stems, 1 mozzarella, 4 desalted anchovy fillets, oil for frying, 1 egg (optional), flour, sparkling mineral water

Clean the flowers, remove the pistils and part of the stem. Slice the mozzarella into cubes and halve the anchovy fillets. Stuff each flower with half an anchovy and a little mozzarella, without overfilling them. Press to close, and dip each flower in the batter that you will have made with (icy) mineral water, flour and an egg (optional). Deep fry the flowers in very hot oil for a few minutes, then drain on paper towels. Serve hot and crisp after sprinkling with a pinch of salt.

Shop in the most sensuous boutique in town

ZouZou is not just a shop, it is a sophisticated and attractive space where fragrances exalt the senses and our imagination is stimulated by the beauty and design of the articles and objects. Just off the Piazza Navona in the heart of Rome, this temple of sensuality is open to all women looking for the most exclusive creations in lingerie and luxury sex toys – precisely those made famous to the public by celebrities such as P. Diddy, Kate Moss, and Eva Longoria, to name just a few.

Discover Chloe Hambel, the young designer of the label Lascivious, the most popular lingerie among ZouZou customers. Or Betony Vernon, the extraordinary, striking creator of erotic jewelry, whose pieces may also be worn "normally". The boutique's pride and joy is the little dressing room decorated by Rafael Vanegas. His work, an expression of desire and eroticism, cultivates the female icon from Renaissance to Pop Art.

For those of you who are about to marry, ZouZou also organizes unforgettable bachelorette parties with aphrodisiac aperitifs that include bubbly wines and finger food, followed by a sensuous journey into the world of ZouZou. The future bride is accompanied to the dressing room and "forced" to change into three honeymoon outfits: the burlesque, the fetish and the romantic bride. Each time the future bride comes out, she will be coached by a burlesque artist on all of the ironic and sexy ways to take them off (gloves, bodice, stockings, etc.)... Whether you are a future bride or simply curious about this provocative world, liberating your sensuality and crossing the threshold of this boutique will definitely make you just a little more mischievous. You will see love in a totally new and stimulating way.

ZOUZOU
Vicolo della Cancelleria, 9A
Tel. +39 06 6892176
www.zouzoustore.com – onlinestore@zouzou.it
Monday 2:00 pm to 7:30 pm
Tuesday to Saturday 11:00 am to 7:30 pm
Closed on Sundays

I'm the typical girl
every mother would
warn you about.

Dita Von Teese

Take a quick trip to the West Coast and back again

Some people adore this spot for its original bar and professional bartenders, who make highly original cocktails with acrobatics and a smile; others love it for its cool summer garden, where you can dine so beautifully amidst lights, fragrances and colors; or others because they've spent so many wonderful evenings just talking, laughing, dreaming and reminiscing there, that they feel completely at home. **Duke's** is definitely a very special place, one that wins the heart of anyone who spends an evening there. If the walls could talk, they would certainly have many stories to tell of romances that began there, or the habits of the stars who love to come and relax, or quite simply, of the warm evenings spent between old and new friends. Trying to find a label for Duke's is impossible. It is forever changing, evolving with each occasion.

The atmosphere resembles a dynamic and refined Californian restaurant (inspired by the concept of fine casual dining), yet it is devoid of any formalism or constraints. Its international cuisine is one of the best in the city, as is its wine cellar, with its impressive selection of wines from all over the world (which are also for sale online). A suggestion: go for happy hour, or a special dinner, or a cocktail with friends, and let yourself enter the West Coast scene. Whether you decide to sit at a table or at the long winding bar, leave all your worries behind. Have fun choosing your favorite songs with your smartphone (You can access Duke's playlist using the wi-fi and select it from your own cell phone, just like a modern jukebox). Order a cocktail that reflects your personality and enjoy being admired in that dress you've worn specially for the occasion. In short, sit back and relax, as any American pilot would say: enjoy a short and unexpected trip to California right in Rome's Parioli neighborhood. As you leave, you'll be asking yourself, "Am I in Rome or West Hollywood?"

DUKE'S INTERNATIONAL RESTAURANT & BAR
Viale Parioli, 200
Tel. +39 06 80690143
www.dukes.it

Take
Bikram Yoga classes

"*Mens sana in corpore sano*" said Decimo Giunio Giovenale, the Roman poet and orator who lived in the years around 100 A.D. And indeed, caring for our bodies is of utmost importance. Roman cuisine is splendid and the tempting traditional dishes are infinite. Yet it is also very rich. So, once we've satisfied out palates, let's think about our figures! If you happen to be in the Vatican area, don't miss the chance to practice what is considered a real must for well-being: Bikram Yoga. This consists of a dynamic sequence of 26 positions and 2 breathing exercises, all done in a heated (40° C) and humid (40% relative humidity) room. So be prepared to sweat! Scientific studies have proven how beneficial perspiring is for the body and the mind. It helps to eliminate mercury, pesticides, weed killers, and all those chemical substances that our body accumulates through food, drink and the air we breathe. The warm temperature also keeps our muscles limber during the exercises, and allows for more intense and extended stretching.

Indeed, the various positions target each of your muscles, organs and glands for a few seconds at a time, reactivating blood circulation, revitalizing cells, strengthening the vertebrae, and relaxing the mind. Students of all levels are welcome. These Bikram Yoga lessons (named after the creator of the method, Bikram Choudhury) are open to all, even to those who are just curious! If this is your first lesson, don't worry: your coordination will improve with time and you will gradually master all of the exercises. What is important is to remember to drink lots of water and to bring a large beach towel with you (the center also has towels you can rent or buy). The lesson lasts ninety minutes and the body gets a complete workout. You will leave feeling totally energized and bursting with new enthusiasm.

Some advice:
• avoid eating in the two hours preceding the lesson;
• keep your body well hydrated throughout the day;
• wear light clothing.

YOGA BIKRAM ROMA
Via Aurelia, 190B (Vatican area)
Tel. + 39 06 39366357
info@bikramyogaroma.it
www.bikramyogaroma.it

Step back in time

Remember that cool leather jacket that the blond girl in the Parioli restaurant was wearing that looked so worn and comfortable? Or those butterfly sunglasses that you looked for everywhere but could not find in any of the shops? Or that sixties damask stole that would have been perfect with your new dress? To find all of these things and more, you'll need to head to Via del Governo Vecchio, a street renowned for its second-hand shops. Though it is just off Piazza Navona, right in the center of Rome, this is off the beaten path and you're unlikely to find it in many tourist guides. Here you'll find everything imaginable in the way of vintage clothes and accessories. If you're a film buff, you can stop at the **Altroquando**, a bookshop that specializes in cinema. In addition to technical texts on filmmaking and screenwriting, it has a superb collection of rare posters and stills from legendary films just begging to be framed. Another interesting stop is **Cinzia al 45**. And, don't forget to have a look at the very British **Penny Lane**.

We'll leave the rest up to you – and those bargain prices!

CINZIA AL 45
Via del Governo Vecchio, 45
Tel. +39 06 6832945

ALTROQUANDO
Via del Governo Vecchio, 80
Tel. +39 06 6879825

PENNY LANE
Via del Governo Vecchio, 4
Tel. +39 06 68892414

Learn to walk on cobblestones in very high heels

Rome's center is characteristically paved with little blocks of leucite known as *sampietrini*. They usually measure 12x12x6 centimeters and, when placed next to one another, can cover very large areas. These cobblestones are not cemented into place, but are hammered into a bed of sand instead.

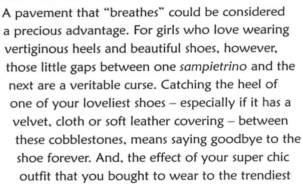

A pavement that "breathes" could be considered a precious advantage. For girls who love wearing vertiginous heels and beautiful shoes, however, those little gaps between one *sampietrino* and the next are a veritable curse. Catching the heel of one of your loveliest shoes – especially if it has a velvet, cloth or soft leather covering – between these cobblestones, means saying goodbye to the shoe forever. And, the effect of your super chic outfit that you bought to wear to the trendiest

restaurant in the center, or to that long-awaited important party, will be completely ruined.

Not to mention the risk of possible sprains or a terrible fall!

After years of testing, it has been proved that there is a way to avoid all of these hazards without giving up wearing those favorite pumps. The secret is to take regular steps, each one equal to about three or four *sampietrini* each. Let us explain: if you start by centering your heel on the first cobblestone and then continue in regular steps, you should be able to balance on the stones without getting a heel stuck in one of the gaps. After that, it is just a matter of having quick enough reflexes to avoid any possible holes or bumps along the way, but these are dangers you might encounter on any asphalt road too.

Despite these tactics, if you still cannot manage, then the only thing left to do is either to walk on your tiptoes, or else to ask your partner for his arm. After all, is there anything more romantic?

Fall in love
watching a sunset over the sea

If there is one thing that makes Rome more appealing than some other cities, it is surely its close proximity to the sea. Some neighborhoods are only a few minutes' drive from the beach, and these were veritable resort towns during the sixties.

Today things have changed somewhat, but the Romans' passion for the sea has remained as intense as ever. Any occasion is good enough to go to the seaside for *spaghetti alle vongole* (spaghetti with small clams) at any of the many restaurants along the coast. And, when the first signs of spring appear, there is not a soul who would not brave the traffic, by car or scooter, to enjoy those first rays of sun at one of the many beach resorts.

Every year, they lounge in the sun, play beach sports, or simply relax there. Every respectable Roman has at least one love story or adventure that blossomed there. Everyone is on holiday, even though they're only minutes from the city.

It would be impossible to list all of these establishments. And though everyone has his or her own favorite place, there is definitely one essential stop for all Fregene regulars, and that is the **Singita**.

Rather than a beach resort per se, the Singita is a special meeting place where the setting sun is celebrated as a spectacular and unique moment. In the evening, the decor of the Singita is suddenly transformed and the beach becomes a huge lounge: the folding chairs are put away, and great lengths of white cloth are put down on the sand, with cushions and low Indonesian tables. This is the suggestive setting for the rite of the sunset every evening. As the warm red summer sun dips into the intense blue of the sea, an Indian man sounds a gong in homage to this splendid natural spectacle: the end of day, and the magical arrival of night. If you would like to continue the evening by having dinner at a good restaurant, **Da Rosario** is the place to go. The restaurant's fine cuisine and fresh seafood, served on its terrace overlooking the sea, will be an unforgettable gourmet experience.

SINGITA
Via Silvi Marina (Fregene)
Tel. +39 06 61964921
www.singita.it

RESTAURANT ROSARIO
Lungomare di Levante, 52
Albos beach resort (Fregene)
Tel. +39 06 66560539

And anyway, all of the I LOVE YOUs
in the world could never equal a
"I find you've lost weight".

Anonymous

Amaze yourself with the optical illusions of the city

Now we would like to take you to three very curious places in Rome where you will witness the most amazing phenomena. Don't worry girls, you haven't had one cocktail too many, these are only optical illusions!

Saint Peter's Basilica: Big and Small

Go to Via Piccolomini, a panoramic road not far from the Aurelia Antica. As you go down this street, leaving the Villa Pamphili behind you, the splendid view of Saint Peter's dome will suddenly loom up and dominate the view. The dome will appear very near and it seems only a few steps away. Try walking towards the Basilica with your eyes constantly fixed on it. At a certain point, you will see that the dome is no longer as big as it was. Though you are drawing closer, due to a strange phenomenon, it quickly grows smaller and smaller until it seems very distant. How is this possible? It is simply an optical illusion.

At first, Saint Peter's Basilica is framed by the buildings and the view of the dome is clear. However, as you gradually approach it, the view begins to include all of the surrounding elements in the landscape. Your brain starts to draw comparisons with everything that surrounds the great dome. It reworks the real dimensions of the Basilica, transmitting the correct data to your eyes.

Saint Peter's Basilica through a keyhole

The Villa del Priorato di Malta is located on the Aventine Hill, just after the Giardino degli Aranci. It is the historic site of the Grand Priory of Rome of the Sovereign Military Order of Malta.

There is a very famous grand door at 3 Piazza dei Cavalieri di Malta. This is an extraordinary little eighteenth-century square in rococo style with decorations that depict the deeds of the Knights of Malta. As you peer through the keyhole of the main door of the Villa, you will see the perfectly framed image of the dome of Saint Peter's Basilica.

The forced perspective of Borromini's Galleria

Palazzo Spada houses the private collection of Cardinal Bernardino Spada. This consists of seventeenth-century paintings, sculptures, ancient furnishings and furniture.

When you cross the inner courtyard of the Palazzo, you will see the famous forced perspective Galleria by Borromini (1652-1653) on your left. This masterpiece is a magnificent combination of art, architecture and mathematics. Here, you will discover that distances, dimensions and depth are completely illusory. Thanks to an amazing optical illusion, you find yourself facing a corridor that appears to be about 40 meters long. It is lined with Doric columns, which converge upon a statue of a Roman warrior that appears to be life-size. In actual fact, however, the corridor is only about 9 meters long, and the statue is no more than 60 cm tall. How is this possible?

Instead of being parallel, the planes of the colonnade actually converge towards a single vanishing point. The height of the columns progressively diminishes, and the columns themselves get closer and closer together. The mosaic pavement tilts upwards. The cardinal thus used the artifice of Baroque art – which tricks the senses – as a moral lesson in the illusory quality of earthly grandeur.

Discover vintage at the table

Romans may remember things from another era like VoV bottles, or the tin boxes that Rossana candies came in, or the bread that was served in taverns and was either wrapped in paper or kept in a tin box. Meat slicers were so cumbersome and odd in those days that they looked more like great monsters. In the heart of Rome's Monteverde Nuovo neighborhood there is a restaurant dedicated to these bygone days.

As you enjoy the good old-fashioned cuisine, you can travel back in time and discover the amusing collection of objects that a group of young people (who have a passion for the fifties) have gathered to decorate their restaurant **Retro 02**. If your Roman friends are too young to remember these cult objects, this will be an excellent occasion to relive some of Rome's retro past. The design of a bygone era – still so captivating today – will bring a smile to your lips as you savor one of the homemade dishes from Retro 02's delicious menu. The day's specials are diligently handwritten on the various blackboards, just like in the old days.

A bonus: don't miss the golden (in all ways!) opportunity of being waited on by one of the fascinating guys dressed in a typical fifties shirt. Everyone is so nice, let them pamper you. Just a tip: go at least once with a girlfriend! Be careful though: the risk of being struck... by lightning... is great indeed.

Need we say more?

RETRO 02
Viale dei Colli Portuensi, 172
Tel. +39 06 53273530
www.trattoriaretro.it

Visit the smallest country in the world

Entrance into Vatican City is not usually permitted, but there are rare exceptions when it is possible to visit certain areas. An exception is made for those who want to go to the **farmacia del Vaticano**. If you need to buy medicines that cannot be found elsewhere, or are simply looking for beauty products and cosmetics, the secret doors to Vatican City will magically open for you. All you need is a prescription. Head to the Porta Angelica, located on Via di Porta Angelica. There, if you show the prescription and an I.D., you will be given a pass to enter and go to the pharmacy.

A word of warning though: the pass is only valid for the pharmacy. So, no straying once you're inside. As you can buy the most prestigious cosmetics at bargain prices there, you'll be tempted to buy up all there is! Be sure to set your budget before leaving.

Your heart will skip a beat as you pass a Swiss guard, who might throw you a glance from under his plumed helmet while feigning complete indifference. Whatever the case may be, at least you can say that you once visited the smallest country in the world!

VATICAN

Via di Porta Angelica, Entrance Porta Sant'Anna
Weekday opening hours: 8:30 am to 6:00 pm; Saturday: 8:30 am to 1:00 pm
Summer opening hours (from 1 July to 31 August): 8:30 am to 3:00 pm;
Saturday: 8:30 am to 1:00 pm
www.vaticanstate.va/IT/Servizi/FarmaciaVaticana

Dress in the fabrics
of famous costume designers

There's a place facing the temple ruins of Largo Argentina that will spark your imagination and inspiration if you're looking for original dress material or special fabric for upholstering. This shop is famous for having fabrics that will express your wildest ideas; your wardrobe will be unique and your house will be one-of-a-kind! The **Azienda Tessile Romana** has fabrics for any dress, upholstery, linen, draping, curtain – and more – on earth. These will be shown to you on the shop's historic original counters, which date back to the turn of the last century.

Indeed, the history of this business started in 1907, when signor Achille decided to move from Naples to Rome with his seven children. The vivid memories of the present owner, a descendent of grandfather Achille, recall the entire history of the business, the family and all the people who have worked there. In addition to being the place for any Roman who wants to give full vent to their boundless creativity, the Azienda has supplied cinema's most demanding costume designers: maestro Piero Tosi, Luchino Visconti's legendary designer, who created the historic costumes for *Il Gattopardo*; and Danilo Donati, costume designer for Federico Fellini's *Amarcord* and *Casanova*. More recently, Maurizio Millenotti drew inspiration there for his costumes for Mel Gibson's *The Passion of the Christ*;

the costumes for Michele Placido's *Romanzo Criminale*, Ettore Scola's *Gente di Roma*, Woody Allen's *To Rome with Love*, and so many more...

Of course, you don't have to be making a movie to find what you need at this amazing shop!

AZIENDA TESSILE ROMANA
Via San Nicola de' Cesarini, 13
Tel. +39 06 68805192 / +39 06 68805197
info@aziendatessile.it

Put light on your wrists

Take Swarovski crystals in the most fashionable colors and stones and textiles of the finest quality. Let gifted, trained hands assemble them into beautiful harmonies to make totally handcrafted creations. These will become the Swarovski luxury *bijoux* that every girl would love to wear.

Even if you usually wear understated accessories and precious jewels, the fascinating, original appeal of a Swarovski bracelet will be irresistible. In the summer, on bare arms and with a light colorful dress, or worn simply with that great T-shirt, the bracelet will bring that touch of precious elegance to your casual look. In the winter, with a sheath dress, or simply worn over the cuff of a blouse, the bracelet will draw the eyes of all the women around you.

WHITE FASHION ROMA
Via di Villa Severini, 54
Tel. +39 06 3291908 / +39 345 8252221
www.whitefashionroma.com

Have someone tell you the story of the *palazzo*, the tower, and the monkey

Strolling through the streets of the center, at 18 Via dei Portoghesi, you will find yourself before the **Palazzo Scapucci**, which takes its

name from the family that owned the edifice during the sixteenth and seventeenth centuries. This Renaissance building is characterized by the **Torre dei Frangipane**, a medieval structure that became famous through a curious anecdote about a monkey named Hilda. Apparently the Scapucci family had an exotic monkey named Hilda for a pet. One day, out of jealousy or maternal instinct, Hilda took the infant Scapucci in her arms and carried him up to the very top of the tower. None of the servants could do anything to stop Hilda, and when the parents of the child returned home, they found their little boy in the arms of the monkey, who was perched at the highest point of the tower. Terrified that the baby might plunge to his death, they exhorted the Virgin Mary to return the child to them unharmed. They vowed that they would build a tabernacle in her honor.

When the father whistled to Hilda to come down, she obediently descended from the tower and placed the little Scapucci child safely at his father's feet.

This is why today, at the top of the Torre dei Frangipane, at the exact spot where Hilda is believed to have taken the child, a statue of Our Lady stands, adorned with the crest of the Scapucci family (a half moon and a star) and an eternal flame. Future owners will be obliged to keep the flame lit, or they will lose their right to the property.

Note: While you're in the area, go and track down Caravaggio's famous works in the churches of Sant'Agostino, San Luigi dei Francesi and Santa Maria del Popolo. You will be able to admire three of Caravaggio's masterpieces: the *Madonna dei Palafrenieri*, *Conversione di San Paolo* and *Vocazione di San Matteo*.

PALAZZO SCAPUCCI
Via dei Portoghesi, 18

Confide in a girlfriend over brunch

The everyday frenzy of our lives constantly presents us with new romantic, professional, or family experiences. And there just never seems to be enough time to share all of the stories and news of our lives with our many girlfriends.

The perfect solution is to catch up on all of our latest titillating emotions while having brunch together at the **Open Colonna**, located on the upper floor of the Palazzo delle Esposizioni.

This is a 2000 m2 greenhouse designed by architect Paolo Desideri, and is a quiet, elegant and luminous space, all in white, which creates an intense harmony of contemporary design, late nineteenth-century architectural

elements, and all the stories and secrets you are dying to share with your friends. Here, everything will have a new flavor, especially thanks to the delicious gourmet ideas by chef Antonello Colonna, a wonderful host whose talent has gained an immediate following among the finest gourmet palates of Rome. Chef Colonna's cuisine reinvents traditional dishes in the light of today's most sophisticated gastronomic habits and trends.

The many buffet dishes are all beautifully presented and delicious. For vegetarians and non-vegetarians, the buffet offers such a wide selection of appetizers, hors d'oeuvres, first and second courses and side dishes that it is impossible not to find something to your liking. Not to mention the desserts, which are irresistible!

Just let yourself enjoy this moment of pleasure and relaxation, and choose which culinary journey you would like to take. They are as multi-faceted as the personality of every woman. As you leave the Open Colonna, don't forget to visit the Arion bookshop on the ground floor. It is considered one of the twenty most beautiful bookshops in the world. It covers approximately 450 m2 and is entirely dedicated to books, catalogues (also of current exhibitions), magazines, music CDs and DVDs on international and Italian art, architecture and design.

OPEN COLONNA
c/o Palazzo delle Esposizioni
Scalinata di via Milano, 9A
Tel. +39 06 47822641
www.opencolonna.it/home.asp
Closed: Mondays and Sunday evenings – Holiday season: August

ARION ESPOSIZIONI BOOKSHOP
via Milano, 15/17
Tel. +39 06 48913361

When I die,
just bring me a coffee,
and you'll see I'll be resuscitated
like Lazarus.

Eduardo De Filippo

Feel like a star in a presidential suite

How do you imagine a presidential suite to be?
What features would it have to make you feel like a star, at least for one night? The answers can all be found at the **Bernini Bristol Luxury Hotel**, located on Piazza Barberini in the very center of Rome.
A modern and refined style with colorful touches that warm the atmosphere and make the suite feel cozy.
A comfortable living area with a big sofa where you can relax, listen to music or leaf through a fashion magazine. A candid double bedroom with a fabulous en suite bathroom equipped with Turkish bath, hydromassage and a huge mirror where you can put your make-up on.
A personal fitness area with all the modern equipment, which leads directly to a private swimming pool with hydromassage, all located on the huge terrace that is for your exclusive use only. And the gorgeous view from the big windows all around the suite: a sweeping panorama of incomparable beauty all the way from the Quirinale to Saint Peter's Basilica.
What more could you desire than to be able to enjoy a hydromassage in your private pool while admiring all the beauties of Rome, or relax in the solarium while sipping your drink?
There's always a special occasion in your life that deserves such an experience: the farewell to single life, a night of romance with the

man of your dreams, a private party with your best girlfriends.
It's up to you to find the perfect occasion. And, if you seize the right
moment, you might even be pleasantly surprised at the accessible rates
of such a unique experience. Nevertheless, if you still haven't found
the right occasion to offer yourself this pleasure, you can still dream a
little beneath the hotel's roof garden. You will have the same view as
you sip an aperitif from its panoramic bar.

BERNINI BRISTOL LUXURY HOTEL
Piazza Barberini, 23
Tel +39 06 488931 / Fax +39 06 4824266
reservationsbb@sinahotels.com

Conquer the heart
of a hardened bachelor

Rome is swarming with hardened bachelors who can make any woman fall hopelessly in love, and who break hearts at the drop of a hat. But is there any way to make one of them fall in love with you? Here are a few useful tips.

The first step is to establish his profile, since the advice we are about to give you can only be applied to someone who perfectly corresponds to the identikit of the hardened bachelor.

Here are his characteristic traits:

1. Allergic to marriage or to living with anyone;
2. A cell phone filled with numbers of women who call him night and day;
3. Tremendously charismatic and just nice enough;
4. Sociable and has lots of buddies;
5. Has an interesting job, an *Easy Rider* motorcycle or Spider, or a house right out of a glossy magazine.

What girl hasn't lost her head, at least once in her life, for a man like this! Unfortunately, the subject in question is perfectly aware that he is extremely desirable, and that is why he always has so many women in his life. He might decide to go to bed with the blonde or ask the brunette out to dinner, yet still not have the slightest intention of committing himself to either one of them.

Yet, one day or another, one woman will finally succeed in calling him her own. Here are some ingredients that might help you to slowly simmer him until he's well done:

1. Air: Let him breathe, make him think he's free;
2. Laughter: When you go out together you're always brilliant, funny, happy, and never boring or predictable;
3. Chase: Be the prey, make him chase you, you'll completely throw him as he won't be used to it;
4. Patience: If you don't want to see him turn and run, try to contain your desire for a wedding ring, and carefully avoid launching into any conversations about marriage or children. These are subjects that terrify any man, so imagine the effect on a hardened bachelor;

5. Rationality: Since we're talking about a hardened bachelor here, he will have had dozens of women before you in his life. So, be impermeable to jealousy, don't try to spy on him or look for clues as to the kind of women who came before you. The best way to fight jealousy is not to have a rival. So, don't create one in your head. After all, if he's dating you now and has dropped all the other women, there must be a reason;

6. Pause: Avoid going out with him every day, or making him think you want to be with him all the time. Leave him the time and space for his manly activities such as his football tournaments, weekly poker games, watching his favorite team on TV and so forth;

7. Activities: Continue to cultivate your own interests, keep yourself busy with the things you've always done: gym, music, manicures;

8. Self-confidence: Always be sure of yourself, even when you're caught off-guard. If he has chosen you, you must definitely have something special. When you're with him, walk with your head high, a radiant smile and a sure step, walk as if you were the only woman on earth;

9. Appearance: Always be well groomed, elegant and fashionable, but without overdoing it with labels or constant shopping sprees. Remember that men are terrified at the idea of supporting a woman with excessively expensive tastes;

10. Independence: Always give him the impression that you are independent, that you know how to take care of yourself. This will be another way of disarming him.

Then, if after all of these efforts you still don't see the slightest signs of him yielding, then be critical, analyze him very well before getting hooked and letting him lead you on for years. Find the courage to go on, unless you can accept being ditched...

Go shopping
in an art gallery

The **White Gallery** is located in the modern EUR part of Rome, an area famous for the rationalist architecture that characterized the thirties. The White Gallery occupies one of the buildings of the Palazzo dell'Arte Moderna. The Lifestyle Store immediately strikes you as a very unique place. Here, the art of living is on show! A gallery that becomes a theatre of new trends and an expression of new concepts in shopping. This is achieved through a multi-sensorial journey, as fascinating as it is ambitious, in which every article, object, garment and accessory carries a powerful communicative charge. The five thousand square meters distributed on three floors interpret luxury in its most modern form, as the search for personal pleasure through the free expression of one's unique style.

You will find various departments: Lifestyle, Kids, Accessories, Women's Daywear, Bijoux, Women's and Men's Fashion Wear, and Classic Collections. There are also several interesting areas that are not to be missed such as The Hall, Fragrances, and Tailoring.

The Hall is structured like an art gallery, with showcases that exhibit the best pieces. In this space, where installations periodically dazzle you with design creations, accessories and fragrances, the many new styles and fashion and communication trends all converge. The Fragrances area is a must-see. Here you will discover fragrances from ancient or artisan traditions as well as very rare and exclusive perfumes and cosmetics. Your senses will discover unique essences and perfumes that can fulfill all needs, from those for the body to those for the home.

Finally, on the first floor, the "Aquarium" absolutely cannot to be missed. Here, expert seamstresses make made-to-measure creations from a simple piece of fabric. Still not enough? Watch for the opening of Finest Food and the Beauty & Relax area. May splendor be with you!

WHITE GALLERY – THE LIFESTYLE STORE
Piazza Guglielmo Marconi, 18/19
Tel. +39 06 54277400
info@whitegallery.it
Commercial: buyer@whitegallery.it
Events: events@whitegallery.it

Escape Rome
on the Isle of Ponza

The island of Ponza is a refuge for Romans who want to reach a spectacular seaside destination quickly for a break from the frenetic and chaotic life of the city. Being in Ponza on June 29th, the feast day of patron saints Peter and Paul, is a tradition not to be missed. All the chic girls know this is the coolest place to be.

How do you get there?

From Termini train station, take the train from Rome to Anzio, or else drive to Anzio.

Once you are at the port of Anzio, take the hydrofoil (about a one-hour crossing) or the ferry (almost two hours) to Ponza. You will arrive on the liveliest side of the island. The port of Ponza reflects the purest example of Bourbon architecture and dates back to the last half of the 1700s. It also has wharves and piers where you will see the splendid yachts that have the Italian and international jet set on board.

Before you decide what to do, be sure to get lunch.

There are many little shops near the port that sell pizza, fruit and pastries. If you want a sure bet, go to the fruit and grocery store run by signora Lina near the café Tripoli. Every year she is there, serving her excellent products to her customers.

Ask her why the shop is called **La Savana** and she'll be delighted to tell you how it all started, as she prepares sandwiches with excellent cured meats, delicious *mozzarella di bufala* or with anything else you might fancy.

What to do by boat?

At the port you can rent a fishing boat or a rubber dinghy, with or without a skipper, and spend the day immersed in the turquoise sparkling sea. Go and see Cocò, who in winter performs with a theatre company that puts on shows for the local people. Not only will he take you on a visit of the island and its caves, he will also tell you lots of stories about Ponza, as only an actor could do.

As you leave the port, to your right you will see the famous Grotte di Pilato, with the connecting ancient Roman *murenario*, the Faraglioni di Calzone Muto, Punta della Guardia, with its imposing and suggestive Faro, the beach of Chiaia di Luna, with its stunning rock wall over the sea, the Grotte di Capo Bianco, the Faraglioni and the Lucia Rosa beach. Then you will come to the natural pools of Cala Feola, Cala dell'Acqua, Punta Papa, Cala Fonte and Cala Felce.

As you leave the port, this time on your left you will come upon the very famous Frontone beach, known for its aperitifs, then Core beach, with its great heart-shaped rock, Cala Inferno, with its relic of a sunken merchant vessel (the *Maria Costanza*), the Arco Naturale, where you can make a wish as you pass beneath it, and Cala Gaetano.

Because of the island's configuration, there is always an area that is protected from the wind and where waters are calm.

A very economical solution is to take a tourist excursion of Ponza and Palmarola with the big boats docked at the port.

What to do on foot?

Rent a little scooter or a little colorful car to get around the island more conveniently and stop wherever you like.

It is easy to get to the Chiaia di Luna beach on foot, and there is a tunnel dating back to Roman times that leads to the beach. Want to go to extremes? Follow the path that leads to the Faro di Monte La Guardia!

Take the bus as a convenient way to get to the other side of the island, to Le Forna and the natural pools of Cala Feola.
An alternative would be to take the taxi boats for a few Euros. They will drop you off at various beaches such as Frontone. When you are facing this beach, if you look up to the right you will see the restaurant **da Gerardo**. It is a bit of a hike up there, but it is

well worth it – not only because of the view of the bay and Ponza's typical pastel houses on the horizon, but also because of the wonderful homemade dishes you can have in the shade of the pergola. The *bruschette* and typical local vegetable soups are not to be missed, nor are the chickling peas or lentils. It's even possible to visit a little museum there and sunbathe on lounge chairs, play cards, or other table games, all for free.

Aperitifs!

When it's aperitif time, all of the Romans gather at the Frontone, the Melograno at the **Grand Hotel Santa Domitilla**, or the Terrazze Kibar at the **Grand Hotel Chiaia di Luna**.

Everyone dances, eats, drinks, goes swimming, and has fun as the music plays on. Do you just feel like something quiet? Go to the Chiaia di Luna beach and enjoy the extraordinary romantic sunset amidst the peaceful lapping of the waves.

Where to eat?

There are countless good places to dine on Ponza, but there are a few restaurants that simply must not be missed because of their excellent cuisine and stupendous location. After that, it's up to you to choose what best suits your taste and mood.

Acqua Pazza, with its beautiful view overlooking the port, is definitely a top-class restaurant. With its white linen tablecloths and teak furniture, it

combines a refined atmosphere with cuisine that uses only the best local seafood. Since 1989, it has been the favorite place of the island's VIPs, as well as Ponza's only Michelin-starred restaurant. (*Very chic*).

Gennarino a Mare is midway between the port of Ponza and Santa Maria, and is built on wooden piles over the sea facing the port. The cuisine is great and typically Mediterranean. (*A great classic*).

Il Tramonto is located on the other side of the island and you can make an excursion there by driving over in one of the colorful cars for rent. The sunset from here is truly sensational, with Palmarola and San Felice Circeo on the horizon... be sure to take your camera! (*Very romantic*).

Pensione Silvia is on the Santa Maria beach, and is very simple and comfortable. Its location is definitely much quieter than the port, though it is only a 15 minute walk away. Amidst the little boats drawn up along the beach, on a quiet and suggestive veranda, the homemade cooking is done entirely by women. As you enter, you will see rock salt on the floor. It's not superstition; let's just say it's a "Mediterranean habit"!

After dinner

In the evening there's usually the "struscio", or evening stroll, along Via Carlo Pisacane to the various bars such as **Welcome's**, **Tripoli**, and the **Winspeare**, which has live music.

Still not ready to call it a day? If you're lucky, there are the "oneshot" evenings at the Frontone, with dinghy service, or at the Grand Hotel Chiaia di Luna. For the very young, the **Covo NordEst** always stays open.

Where to sleep?

There are many hotels on Ponza, but the Grand Hotel Santa Domitilla is one of the real pearls of the Mediterranean! Peace and relaxation, a refined and beautifully kept environment. Have a warm *ciambellone* just out of the oven for breakfast under the garden pergola, and enjoy a true holiday. Another plus? The fabulous Percorso Benessere in the suggestive Grotte Romane (baths), and the hotel's two seawater pools!
Yet perhaps you'd prefer to experience the island in a much more characteristic way? The inhabitants of Ponza rent out their colorful little pastel houses, or caves transformed into rooms, and many other types of lodging to tourists... The rule is: "Be adaptable!"

Extra

Are you feeling a little daring and want to give a wilder and more original touch to your holiday? Take an excursion to Palmarola! Accessible only by boat or by special arrangement with rental services in Ponza, the island of Palmarola is completely cut off from the world: no electricity, water or telephone.
The island is uninhabited, except – in summer – by the Fendi family (yes, the Italian fashion house!) and by the people who run **O'Francese**, a restaurant with rooms for rent.
Here, a unique experience awaits: bathing in crystalline waters, watching an incredibly romantic sunset, and, after taking a shower amidst the bushes, a dinner of the local fish of the day. When you are totally relaxed, you can switch off some of the only lights on the entire island, so that the sky is just lit by billions of stars! In the total silence, you will fall asleep rocked by the waves...

N.B. Whether you go to Ponza or Palmarola: take low shoes, sun lotion, and a fat wallet!

HYDROFOILS AND FERRIES
LINEE VETOR
Tel. +39 06 9845083
www.vetor.it

CAREMAR
Tel. +39 06 98600083
www.caremar.it
N.B. Booking advisable!

COCÒ
Via Banchina Mamozio
Tel. +39 338 8941314

GROCERY STORES
LA SAVANA
Piazza Carlo Pisacane, 17
Tel. +39 0771 831596

WHERE TO EAT
GERARDO MAZZELLA
Cultural Association and Museum
Via Frontone
Tel. + 39 0771 80009 / +39 339 8491446

ACQUA PAZZA
Piazza Carlo Pisacane, 10
Tel. + 39 0771 80643
acquapazza@ponza.com

GENNARINO A MARE
Via Dante, 64
Tel. +39 0771 80071 / +39 0771 80593
www.gennarinoamare.com

IL TRAMONTO
Via Campo Inglese
Tel. + 39 0771 808563

PENSIONE SILVIA
Via Marina – Tel. +39 0771 80075

BARS & CAFES
WELCOME'S
Piazza Carlo Pisacane
Tel. +39 0771 809823

TRIPOLI
Piazza Carlo Pisacane
Tel. +39 0771 809862

WINSPEARE
Via Banchina Di Fazio
Tel. +39 0771 80533

HOTELS
GRAND HOTEL SANTA DOMITILLA
Via Panoramica
Tel. +39 0771 809951/2/3/4
www.santadomitilla.com

GRAND HOTEL CHIAIA DI LUNA
Via Panoramica
Tel. + 39 0771 80113
www.hotelchiaiadiluna.com

O'FRANCESE (Palmarola)
Tel. + 39 0771 80 080 / +39 081 5261158 / +39 380 2542553
ofrancese@palmarola.org

PONZA INFORMATION
Tel. +39 0771 80031
www.prolocodiponza.it – info@prolocodiponza.it

Try different foods for every season

In the film *Eat Pray Love*, the protagonist Elizabeth Gilbert, played by Julia Roberts, takes a journey to three countries (Italy, India and Bali) in search of herself, the pleasures of life, God and, finally, true love.
In Rome, the protagonist reawakens to life. She realizes she can still wonder at the world thanks to Rome's artistic beauties, *"dolce far niente"* lifestyle, and gorgeous food.
And, indeed, food in the Capital is a veritable cult, with something special for every season.

SPRING:
Day: Frullato
With the first warm days of spring, there is so much to do in the city. A delicious *frullato*, an Italian milkshake, is the perfect drink to boost our vitamins and mineral salts!
The bar **Pascucci** near Torre Argentina boasts at least one hundred kinds of specialties, created over seventy years of activity. The centrifuged smoothies are excellent, but you must also try the *frullati*, such as the *frappè Monterosa* (frothy milk and *amarene* sour black cherries), the *frullato Amalfi* or the *frullato con uovo e marsala* (a real *bomba!*).

Night: Maritozzo con panna

This is a typical Roman sweet, a very light brioche, leavened and baked in the oven, then cut lengthwise and filled with whipped cream. It is said to have originated in ancient Rome when loaves were sweetened with honey and raisins. During the Middle Ages, a future husband would offer his betrothed a *maritozzo*. This perhaps explains its humorous name, though others think it might be because of its rather phallic shape. The nineteenth-century Roman poet, Gioacchino Belli, among other writers in history, has left us a colorful description of this typical pastry. In Trastevere, there's a place called the **Maritozzaro** that has served this lovely specialty to Rome's night owls every evening for the past fifty years.

SUMMER:

Day: Gelato

Avoid the chains that produce ice creams with industrial ingredients. Instead, have a real homemade Italian ice cream made with fresh fruit and quality products!

One of the best ice-cream parlors in Rome is **Giolitti**, located near the Camera dei Deputati and the Pantheon. It all began here in 1890 when Giolitti opened as a simple dairy shop, though it was soon supplying the Royal House itself. Don't be surprised if you think you see Cameron Diaz, Susan Sarandon, Antonio Banderas, Justin Timberlake or other celebrities there – they all know about it!

Another excellent place is **Ciampini**, where homemade ice cream has been produced for over fifty years according to recipes handed down for four generations. Each flavor is balanced separately by a master ice-cream maker. Organic milk, eggs and the best fresh cream are used, and the fruit flavors contain up to 70% fresh fruit!

Would you like to experiment with some daring flavors and combinations? Try **Fatamorgana**. There are delicious inventions such as chocolate and rosemary, pineapple and ginger, raspberry with almonds, vanilla and rice or...

Night: Grattachecca

In the days when there were no freezers or refrigerators, people used a big block of ice called a "checca" to keep food fresh.

And even today, there are still kiosks in Rome that make grattachecche just as they did in the good old days. This is shaved ice which is made by scraping a checca with a special utensil, and then put in a cup and doused with your favorite syrup: mint, sour black cherry, tamarind, melon, etc.

AUTUMN:

Day: Marrons glacés

Giulio **Giuliani**, after a trip to Switzerland in the forties, decided to return to his native Italy and produce genuine homemade candied chestnuts. He opened his Marron Glacé & Cioccolatini in Rome's Prati neighborhood. The art of delicious candied chestnuts is a delight here.

Night: La Cioccolateria

An old chocolate factory with antique engravings on the walls and shelves laden with glass jars, canisters, and old-fashioned tin boxes... And little wooden tables and an ivy pergola in the garden. In Rome's quarter of San Lorenzo, the unique and suggestive atmosphere of this former chocolate factory will satisfy your every craving for something sweet. You will find the best and most fragrant chocolate, served hot with whipped cream, or in many other different ways. The restaurant here is great too.

WINTER:

Day: Pizzette

There is an excellent and very characteristic bakery to discover in Rome's ancient Ghetto neighborhood called **Antico Forno del Ghetto**. The delicious aromas of their little pizzas waft all the way over to Via del Portico D'Ottavia, near the Synagogue. Excellent whether rosso or white, soft or crunchy, try to have them while they're hot.

Night: Filetti di baccalà fritti

Er Filettaro is right off of Campo de' fiori, in a charming little piazza facing Via dei Giubbonari. One of the last bulwarks of traditional Roman cuisine, it specializes in deep-fried cod fillets. They're a little pricey, but great!

PASCUCCI
Via di Torre Argentina, 20
Tel. +39 06 6864816
www.pascuccifrullati.it
Open every day from 6:00 am to 12:00 am

IL MARITOZZARO
Via Ettore Rolli, 50
Tel. +39 347 2175214

GIOLITTI
Via degli Uffici del Vicario, 40
Tel. +39 06 6991243
www.giolitti.it
Opening hours: 7:00 am to 2:00 am

CIAMPINI ROMA
Piazza San Lorenzo in Lucina, 29
Tel. +39 06 6876606
www.ciampini.com

FATAMORGANA
Piazza degli Zingari, 5 / Piazza San Cosimato /
via Roma Libera, 11 / Via Bettolo, 7
info@gelateriafatamorgana.it
www.gelateriafatamorgana.it

LA SORA MARIA DAL 1933 – LA GRATTACHECCA
Via Trionfale, on the corner of Via Bernandino Telesio (Prati)

SORA MIRELLA – LA GRATTACHECCA DAL 1915
Lungotevere degli Anguillara, near Ponte Cestio
(Isola Tiberina)

GRATTACHECCA FONTE D'ORO
Lungotevere Raffaello Sanzio, on the corner with
Piazza Giuseppe Gioacchino Belli (Trastevere)

N.B. The grattachecche kiosks are open at any time
of the day or night.

GIULIANI – MARRONS GLACÉS E CIOCCOLATINI DAL 1949
via Paolo Emilio, 67 – Tel. +39 06 3243548
Opening hours: 8:30 am to 7:30 pm
Sunday: 8:30 am to 1:00 pm

SAID DAL 1923 – ANTICA FABBRICA DEL CIOCCOLATO
Via Tiburtina, 135 (San Lorenzo) – Tel. +39 06 4469204
said@said.it

ANTICO FORNO DEL GHETTO
P.zza Costaguti, 31 – Tel. +39 06 68803012
anticofornodelghetto@hotmail.com

DAR FILETTARO
Largo dei Librari, 88 – Tel. +39 06 6864018
Opening hours: 5:30 pm to 11:10 pm

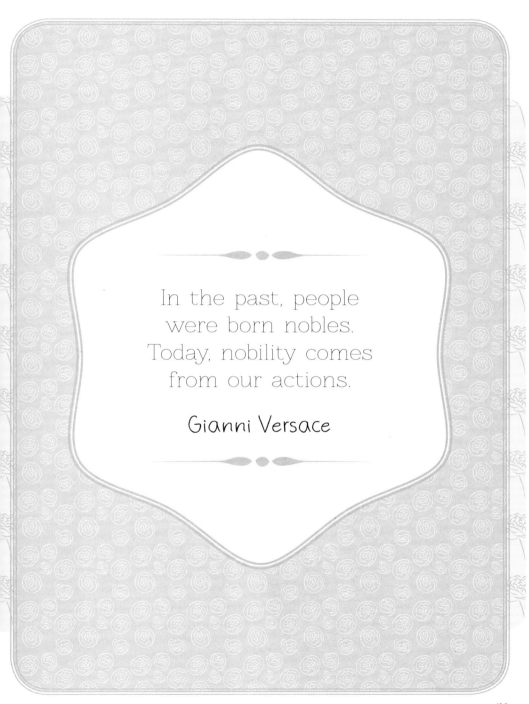

In the past, people
were born nobles.
Today, nobility comes
from our actions.

Gianni Versace

Have a seal ring made with your initials

Once upon a time there was the seal or signet ring...
These rings were widely used in the 1800s, when every wealthy person had a ring with his initials, or the family coat of arms, engraved on it. These rings were used to sign agreements or letters, and to initial such documents as bills, laws or edicts. For pirates, a seal ring would indicate a certain rank of command. The Pope's seal ring, known as the *Anello del Pescatore*, or Fisherman's Ring, indicated the beginning of a Papacy. If a person lost his seal ring, it was considered a real disaster!
Today, individuality is important to us; we have a desire to distinguish ourselves from the mass and leave our own personal stamp. To find a ring that is just as special as we are is not always easy, and perhaps this is the true "disaster". Yet, just as there is always a happy ending to every true fairytale, in Rome there is artist Marco De Luca, who is the knight who will come to your rescue!
You will find his shop, **Toko**, right near Piazza Navona, where he will always be ready to welcome you with his usual helpful and friendly manner.
His designs are a point of reference for famous VIPs and television and film celebrities, including actress Sabrina Impacciatore, singer Emma (who wore his creations at the San Remo Festival too), intellectual columnist Roberto D'Agostino and – drum roll – Ron Woods of the Rolling Stones!
Marco De Luca is an artist who works all different kinds of metals,

he restyles antique jewelry, recovers antique coins and sacred ex voto icons (his great passion is the Sacred Heart) and transforms them into inimitable pieces of highly original jewelry.

Each of his seal rings is entirely handcrafted. There can never be two alike!

This might be just the right way to use those old coins saved from trips abroad. Or, to finally melt down those old gifts from that ex-boyfriend who it is time you forget, launch a new tradition, reproduce the ring of a mysterious great-great-grandmother in a faded photo, or simply give vent to your fantasy through your choice of material, size, color, finish and the style of your initials!

Wearing a signet ring with your initials on your little finger is truly the height of chic. The little finger, traditionally associated with the god Mercury, symbolizes intelligence and strong communicative, intuitive, intellectual and persuasive gifts. Be careful, though, when choosing which hand you will wear your ring on! The right hand, controlled by the left hemisphere of the brain (the one that controls our logic), is the active hand. Its energy emanates outwards and towards others. Wearing a ring on this hand is a sign of awareness, will and control. The left hand, however, is receptive. It is controlled by the creative part of the brain. Wearing a ring on the left hand expresses sensitivity, creativity and emotion.

These characteristics can be an amusing game that helps us understand our state of mind and that of others. And, having a seal ring created for you by an artist such as Marco De Luca will already represent two things for sure: the expression of your personality and an unforgettable memory of Rome.

TOKO
Via del Corallo, 32/33
Tel. + 39 06 68210780 / +39 393 1046762
marcodelucajewels@gmail.com

Find the perfect disguise for a masquerade party

The best place to find everything you need for a Roman masquerade party is **Studio 13**, a veritable treasure of ideas and solutions to make you the star of your costume party!

Disguises, wigs, special effects, accessories, make-up for film, television and photo shoots, and creams to naturally change the color of your skin will all make your evening a tremendous success.

Studio 13 is a space that is specially designed for experimenting with the newest and boldest techniques and ideas. The Studio's make-up artists use quality products that will resist the heat of a crowded club or stand the test of water. The two floors of the Studio are dedicated to making your ideas become reality through special make-up, body painting, airbrush techniques, gadgets and costumes. Just let your inspiration take flight, the Studio's staff will do the rest!

There is also a school inside the Studio that trains professional make-up artists and technicians. So, are you ready for your Jim Carrey evening?!

STUDIO 13
Piazza Cavour, 13
Tel. +39 06 68803977 / +39 06 68130463
info@studio13roma.it
Tuesday to Saturday 10:00 am to 7:30 pm

Have some macarons
sent home

What does a research scientist with two degrees (one in biology and the other in oceanography) and the typical French *macarons* (those perfectly round sweets in a thousand colors and flavors with a soft butter filling), so popular now even in Rome, have in common? Nothing, you would say. But, if the researcher is also a Frenchwoman who has worked for many years in a chemical laboratory (amidst test tubes, elements and compounds), then you might understand how for Laure Sophie Schiettecatte (the creator of **www.macaron.it**), it was only a short hop from the laboratory to fine pastry making and perfect macarons. The result of her experiments is absolutely delicious!

Laure Sophie's macarons are fabulous as much for their quality as they are for their taste. They far surpass the most prestigious Parisian varieties. This has been confirmed by the French Embassy itself, which officially serves L.S. macarons. L.S. macarons range from the most classic kinds such as coffee, caramel, chocolate, coconut, strawberry, lemon, liquorice, and orange, to the most exotic flavors and combinations such as blackberry and violet, mojito, mango, lemon and basil, or chocolate and curcuma. All L.S. macarons are made from quality ingredients, such as Valrhona Extra Amer 67% chocolate, Amarelli powdered liquorice, and Bourbon del Madagascar vanilla. Choose your flavors and your preferred packaging, and enjoy this magical French specialty directly at home, for your birthday party or wedding reception. Indeed, they are only a telephone call away. Oh, just a word of advice. When you call

Laure Sophie, don't expect a gentle young lady with a French accent to answer the phone. Instead, you'll hear the big booming voice of former rugby player, Adriano. So, when placing your order, perhaps it is best to avoid referring to unlikely colors such as mauve, cyclamen, prune or mint green... We all know that any man's chromatic scale leaves much to be desired, so can you imagine a rugby player's?!

MACARON.IT

Tel. +39 06 92937848 / +39 393 6222766

www.macaron.it

Deliver a simple gift in a very special way

How many times have you dreamed of being able to star in one of those great scenes from an American movie? Admit it, when the movie is over, you're invariably caught with a big silly smile stamped on your face. So, get busy, have your gift delivered just as if you were the star of that movie! What the gift is, or how much it costs is of little importance, what counts is how to amaze that special person when he receives it.

"Romantic Comedy"

1. Write a little note to your "man":
   "I'm giving you Rome, since Rome is wonderful, because probably no one else has ever given you this, because wherever you go, Rome satisfies you, because just when you think you've conquered her, you find yourself loving her with all her weaknesses... because you cannot forget her."
   Then, wait for just the right moment to tell him;
2. Blindfold him so that he won't know where you're taking him. Don't lead him straight to the destination, but change the route, take the same streets more than once, go the long way around...;
3. Then lead him to the **Fontanone al Gianicolo** (Gianicolo Fountain) where a stupendous panoramic view of Rome unfolds before you, keeping your back

to the Fontana dell'Acqua Paola, as the Fontanone is also known (Pope Paul V commissioned Giovanni Fontana to design it in 1611-1612);

4. Have him sit in the middle of the terrace, put earphones in his ears and play your chosen song;
5. Take off his blindfold and, once he's admired the panorama, hand him the note;
6. Give him your gift and enjoy watching his reaction.

N.B. Make sure that when you play your song, the volume doesn't burst his eardrums!

"Adventure Film"

1. Reserve the thermal tubs at the beautiful **El** Spa for just the two of you;
2. Arrange with the staff to have your "man" receive his gift on a floating tray while the two of you are in the tub;
3. On the big day, you will be welcomed in the relaxation area with candied fruit and herbal tea. Once in the tub at El, the first floating tray will arrive with two glasses of bubbly and then, another one will float down with your gift for him!

N.B. Do you want to make the surprise even bigger? Give him three little gifts. That way, the tray will come floating down several times, and he'll be endlessly surprised!

"Around the World in 365... Sweets"

This time you'll have fun preparing him a little dinner at home, with all the typical dishes that you've had during your trips together, whether real, imagined, or planned. If you're wondering where to find the rarest and most creative ingredients, you'll find lots of ideas at **Castroni**. This is a chain of shops all over Rome that sells the world's finest specialties.

Sangria with strawberries, apples and oranges (Spain)
Guacamole and nachos, hot spicy sauce, cheese sauce (Mexico)

Couscous (Africa)
Moussakà (Greece)

Roast beef (England) with steamed Brussels sprouts
Goulash (Hungary) with baked potatoes

Lychees (China and Southeast Asia)
Passion fruit (Brazil)

Pastel de Nata (Portugal)
Crepes with Nutella (France)

Merlot, Cabernet, Sauvignon, Pinot nero
Chardonnay (France)
Zinfandel (California)

FONTANA DELL'ACQUA PAOLA OR "FONTANONE"
Via Garibaldi, on a level with no. 35 (Gianicolo area)

EL SPA
Via Plinio, 15 c/d
Tel. +39 06 68192869
mail@elspa.it

CASTRONI
www.castroni.it

Treat yourself to a Roman aperitif in perfectly... Milanese style!

If you are convinced that Milanese aperitifs are unbeatable, then you haven't been to 68 Via Ostiense yet. Among the many places of the Roman "movida" around the Mercati Generali, there is one bar in particular that will make you change your mind and turn your geography upside down when it comes to having a good *aperitivo*. That place is the **Doppiozeroo**! Can you resist the delicious smell of freshly baked bread or pizza and cakes right out of the oven? No (or rather "N-0-0 at the "Double 0-0"!), we don't think so! Apparently these are the kinds of aromas that directly activate the limbic system of our brains and have the power to encourage feelings of well being, a good mood and even... altruism! So, if you pass by Via Ostiense, you'll want to go to the Doppiozeroo and let yourself be carried away by its pleasant and intriguing atmosphere.

Here batches of freshly baked products are served all day long. The space becomes a place for lunch, aperitifs, dinner and, for those who want a late night out, a good night cap and a little music.

Meet your best girlfriend for a drink there, or for a casual dinner. And, don't forget – now that you're feeling so sociable thanks to the smell of the baked bread – to peek around at all the interesting people you might meet at any time of day there! You see, you don't have to go to Milan for a great *aperitivo*!

DOPPIOZEROO
Via Ostiense, 68
Tel. +39 06 57301961

Discover the legend
of the "Fontana delle Tartarughe"

There is an ancient tale about Duke Mattei, whose family can be traced back to one of the oldest lineages of the patricians of Rome. The Duke had such a passion for gambling that he once almost lost his entire fortune in just one evening. When the Duke's future father-in-law heard about this, he immediately broke off the engagement between his daughter and the Duke. However, Mattei, in order to demonstrate his worth and redeem himself, decided to give a reception that would last until dawn. During that time lapse, in just one night, he had a splendid fountain built in front of the palazzo. The morning after the reception, the Duke called his future father-in-law over to the window and declared, "Now just see what the penniless Mattei has been able to do in just a few hours!"

The Duke was once again given his beloved's hand in marriage and, to commemorate these events, he had the window where everyone had come to admire the beautiful Fontana delle Tartarughe walled up.

The fountain dates back to the end of the 1500s, but the turtles that made it famous are said to have been created by Gian Lorenzo Bernini or Andrea Sacchi. Pope Alexander VII had them added to the fountain in the mid-seventeenth century when it was restored.

The turtles have been stolen at various times throughout history: in 1944 the four turtles disappeared, but were all eventually recovered. In 1979, however, they were stolen again, but this time only three were found.

Today, the turtles placed around the fountain are copies. The originals are housed in the Musei Capitolini.

The fountain is so impressive that in the early 1900s William and Ethel Crocker had a life-sized copy built for their villa. In 1954, the family donated this fountain to the city of San Francisco, though it was later moved to Huntington Park.

FONTANA DELLE TARTARUGHE
Piazza Mattei

Learn the seven superstitions of Roman etiquette

Even the coolest Roman girl – so hip on the latest trends that she doesn't *follow* fashion trends, she *sets* them – is inevitably bound to certain traditions handed down by her grandmother and great-grandmother (all Romans born and bred of course!).

Indeed, when it comes to the table, there are certain special rules of etiquette to be observed in Rome, an unwritten code that no one would ever dream of breaking.

Superstition or not, if you want to be perfectly integrated, it is crucial to know these rules if you don't want to commit an unforgivable blunder.

Here are seven rules to always remember:

1. There cannot be thirteen dinner guests at the table, so it is better to opt for finger food or a buffet;

2. Do not place pieces of cutlery on top of one another to form a cross;

3. Do not refold your napkin the way you found it when you sat down to dinner;

4. Never play cards or any other game when the table is set and covered with a tablecloth;

5. When a guest asks you to pass the salt, put the shaker near the person but let the guest pick it up himself;

6. At the end of a dinner, as you leave your host's house, do not put your seat back under the table;

7. When you pour any drink into another guest's glass, whether wine or water, always make sure to fill the glass generously.

Are you curious to know the origin
of these strange habits?
Go to page 188 and find out!

A shopping secret...
right at your fingertips

The pleasure of discovering Rome's little secrets is part of the journey of getting to know the city. Walking through the streets of the center, shopping can be much more than just buying something or casually glancing at a window. **Les Copains** proposes something a bit different at its newly opened shop at 32 via Borgognona, on the corner of Bocca di Leone. Here every detail of this elegant and welcoming space expresses a unique atmosphere that is both classic and modern. All of the super fashionable girls in Rome love this historic Italian label. They know that the most beautiful knitwear in the city can be found at Les Copains, and especially the most elegant and refined cashmere tops...

Yet, a surprise also awaits. How many of you know that you will also be welcomed with a free manicure too? This is what customers will find every first Wednesday of the month.

Between one garment and another, an expert Nail & Beauty team will care for your hands as you discover a selection of exciting nail polishes created exclusively for Les Copains by Morgan Taylor. Definitely an original glamour experience... right at your fingertips!

LES COPAINS
Via Borgognona, 31
www.lescopains.com

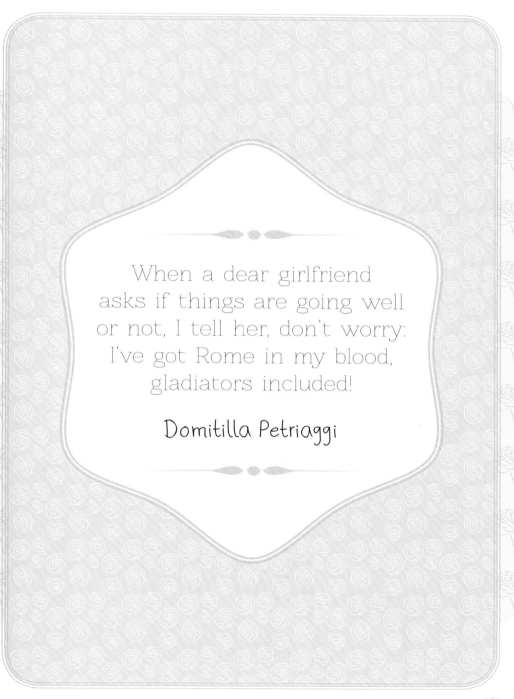

When a dear girlfriend
asks if things are going well
or not, I tell her, don't worry:
I've got Rome in my blood,
gladiators included!

Domitilla Petriaggi

Write a letter on your personalized stationery

Today true luxury is being able to take the time to improve the quality of our lives. Writing a letter means devoting time to expressing our thoughts and feelings. For the person who receives the letter, it will be the pleasure of seeing that you truly care.

There is a lovely little shop near the Pantheon that produces hand-decorated stationery using artistic techniques that have almost completely disappeared in today's world.

Inside the shop, you will discover ancient colors, the smell of forgotten fragrances, and the evocative touch of materials, which will immediately transport you back in time. You will find just the perfect stationery.

You can also watch a rare and fascinating demonstration: the unique process of "marbling", a technique of chromatic decoration that dates back to the seventeenth century and that reproduces the effect of marble on paper.

Your marbled stationery will be unique, classic and timeless. When you have written your letter, put it in a matching envelope and perhaps even choose a lovely collection stamp. Before mailing your letter, be sure to spray a little of your favorite perfume on the envelope. Your unmistakable essence will be there before you!

IL PAPIRO
Via del Pantheon, 50
Tel. + 39 06 6795597
N.B. At this shop you can see
the process of marbling described above
Salita de' Crescenzi, 28
Tel. + 39 06 6868463

Be ready with your overnight bag

You've spent a super evening with your girlfriend in Rome. Aperitifs, a nice dinner, some fun places, lots of chatting, a club... Now it's late, you're exhausted, your girlfriend's house is just around the corner, perhaps it's not really advisable to drive now, so why don't you stay overnight at her place?

Or...

You've just met the Roman boy of your dreams. He struck up a conversation right away and he's so funny. For men like him, quick wit and an answer to everything is second nature! A lot of things have told you that he's very passionate and "*de core*" (has a warm heart). So, you've played with fire all night, and now he suggests you go over to his place, but you... are you really prepared to sleep outside?

Before leaving home (or the hotel), always be sure to have a little "survival kit" with you:

- ✔ Toothbrush and toothpaste;
- ✔ Wet wipes and a change of underwear;
- ✔ Hairbrush and hair tie;
- ✔ Makeup tissues;
- ✔ Mascara, pencil, under eye concealer and lip gloss;
- ✔ Your wonderful personality.

The "morning after", if you look like a zombie (with smudged eyeliner like a panda bear and lipstick smears reminiscent of last night's spaghetti!), your girlfriend will probably just have a good laugh, but your prince charming might get the wrong idea... That evening he had kissed a princess, but in the morning she's turned into a toad!

Enjoy a *cabana* on the beach just like in Miami

Spending a day at the sea, on the historic coast of Ostia, means enjoying a wide range of restaurants, nightclubs, beach resorts, and even a well-equipped marina.

Of course, there are all kinds of beach resorts. If you're looking for something special, try the **V Lounge**, with its unique style and atmosphere.

V Lounge is a good option for those who are looking for a trendy place that offers everything they might desire for a day at the sea. Its all-white decor and green English-style lawn that provides cool relief from the burning sand, recalls the most beautiful hotels in Miami and photos of the international jet set on holiday.

There is something to suit all tastes. You can have an exclusive cabana all to yourself, relax on one of the fabulous lounge chairs in a private area with restaurant service, sunbathe around the beautiful swimming pool, which has its own spa, or even reserve a cabin equipped with hydromassage and plasma TV.

And, if this still isn't enough, you can always call upon the exclusive car valet service, which will take you from your place to the beach, just like a real VIP!

Just let yourself be spoilt and pampered until sunset in this wonderful world, and then your only problem will be to decide which cocktail to order.

V LOUNGE
Lungomare Amerigo Vespucci, 62
Lido di Ostia
Tel. (beach resort) +39 06 56470240
Tel. (restaurant) +39 06 56470171

Know all the best places for Roman pizza

How incredible that just with a little water, flour, salt and yeast you get something as divine as pizza!

The first pizza was created in Naples in the fifteenth century, but Rome also boasts an impressive tradition.

There is a difference between Neapolitan and Roman pizza. The pizza made in Naples has a deep pan crust, its crust is thicker, and it is not baked as long as Roman pizza. Roman pizza has a much thinner crust and is baked at a lower temperature, which makes it crispier.

There are so many great places in Rome to have a good pizza, so don't get caught in a "tourist trap". Whether you want pizza-by-the-slice or not, make sure you choose the right place to have this delicious specialty!

PIZZARIUM
(by the slice)
Via della Meloria, 43
Tel. +39 06 39745416

FORNO CAMPO DE' FIORI
(by the slice)
Campo De' Fiori, 22
Vicolo del Gallo, 14
Tel. +39 06 68806662

LA GATTA MANGIONA
Via Federico Ozanam, 30-32
Tel. + 39 06 5346702

LA FUCINA
Via Giuseppe Lunati, 25/31
Tel. +39 06 5593368

SFORNO
Via Statilio Ottato, 110
Tel. + 39 06 71546118

LA MONTECARLO
Vicolo Savelli, 13
Tel. +39 06 6861877

PIZZERIA AI MARMI
(L'OBITORIO)
Viale Trastevere, 53
Tel. +39 06 5800919

BAFFETTO
Via del Governo Vecchio, 114
Tel. + 39 06 6861617

Take up ten challenges

This page is dedicated to all of those wildly curious enough to take up these 10 little challenges... Have fun!

Go on a
scooter ride
like Audrey Hepburn
in *Roman Holiday*

Learn the names of
Rome's bridges
by jogging
along the Tiber

Visit
Rome's
Rose Garden

Get to know a real
paparazzo of
Rome's *dolce vita*

Walk down
the steps at
Campidoglio in
an evening gown

Admire the
chandelier at
Piazza Mincio

Attend a
wedding at the
Campidoglio

Find out where
Alberto Sordi's
house is

Spot the
grey heron
on Ponte Rotto

Go to see
the azaleas
on Piazza
di Spagna

Take the right gift for that special invitation

If you're reading this chapter, it definitely means that you are now perfectly integrated into Roman life: you've been invited to dinner at a friend's house, or your boyfriend's parents have asked you to come for lunch. And now you're wondering what you can take them as a thoughtful gift. The classic good bottle of wine or nice bouquet of flowers are always appreciated. Yet there are ways to give them a refined and truly original touch so you can leave a wonderful impression!

Idea no. 1

Go to **Bloemen Florist**, where bouquets and floral arrangements have been perfected to a true art! In this tiny little shop, good taste and class produce the most impressive creations. Floral art becomes a rare, elegant and truly original expression.

These creations combine inspired arrangements of rare petals, mosses, branches, barks and blossoms. Bloemen has gained a reputation among celebrities, VIPs and, above all, posh Roman society. It is a good idea to go a few days before your event or appointment to discuss the arrangement that best corresponds to you with the florist designer.

Idea no. 2

Would you like to win the hearts of everyone and add that little touch of fun and exoticism that is such a huge part of your personality? Arrive with an extraordinary bouquet of fresh fruit, as only **EdibleArrangements** knows how to create. Fruit? Yes, that's what we said...

Ready to be even more daring? Ask to have the fruit covered with the finest white, dark, or milk chocolate. It will be a veritable feast for all five senses: the astoundingly beautiful colors; the extraordinary, irresistible fragrance of choice fresh fruit; the delicate, fine chocolate; the tasteful wrapping... You will soon be knocking on their door again – for many more invitations!

Idea no. 3

An excellent bottle of wine can be a truly original gift if it happens to be produced in Lazio. Show you know and appreciate the region's products and pay a compliment to your Roman host by offering a truly exceptional wine. One of the best gifts you can select is definitely a bottle of Mater Matuta (even better if in the exclusive Magnum) from the wine cellar **Casale del Giglio**. Indeed, the award-winning Mater Matuta (the 1996 vintage is one of the best), 85% Syrah and 15% Petit Verdot, is a prestigious, full-bodied ruby red wine. It is fruity and intensely fragrant with a taste of ripe marasca cherries and strong spicy highlights of coriander, nutmeg and cinnamon. Its aroma has complex accents of violet, prune, coffee, thyme, black pepper and musk. In Roman mythology, Mater Matuta was the goddess of the morning or of the dawn. She was the female principle of life that pervades all of Nature, the protectress of fertility, birth, and new life. Offering a wine with a name like this can only augur well!

BLOEMEN FLORIST
Via Terenzio, 37
Tel. +39 06 6892901

EDIBLEARRANGEMENTS
Via Gregorio VII, 328
Tel. +39 06 97611278

CASALE DEL GIGLIO
Via Aventina, 32
Tel. +39 06 5745717
roma@casaledelgiglio.it

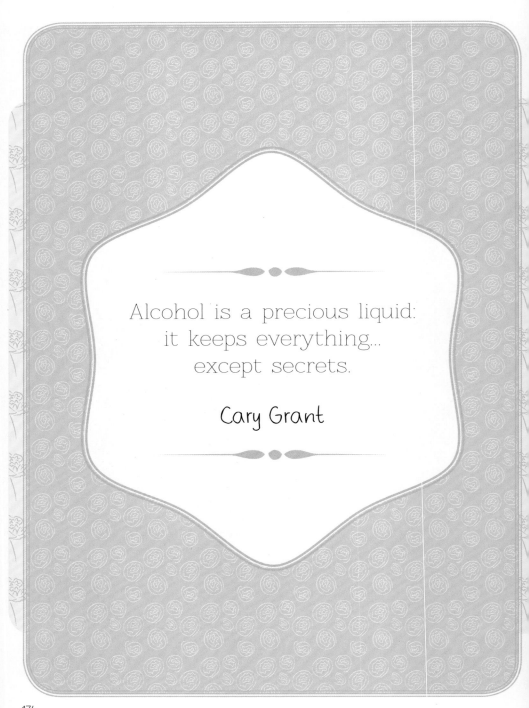

Alcohol is a precious liquid:
it keeps everything...
except secrets.

Cary Grant

Enter the Bermuda Triangle and try to find your way out

The true Bermuda Triangle is actually in Rome, between the **Bar del Fico**, **Jonathan's Angels** and **Les Affiches**. Once you enter this area of Rome you will not want to leave it, especially on warm balmy evenings.

For Romans, any occasion is good enough to sit outside chatting with friends over a tasty cool drink. In fact, in the Capital every corner is a "sitting room" and every angle of the city a grandiose movie set: sunsets that turn the white marble pink, spectacular monuments, historic buildings, and the impressive statues that are so lifelike.

What might be a fascinating tour for a foreign visitor is often just a Roman's usual stroll around the neighborhood where, in just a few steps, he has a complete change of scene, different cafes, groups of friends, and types of evenings. Near Piazza Navona there are three very popular and historic bars, each with its own character and distinctive style.

Entering inside Jonathan's Angels bar is a bit like visiting the house of a narcissistic artist: ornaments, candelabra, highly colorful paintings (which all share a common subject: the bar's owner, a former acrobat and stuntman), photos and figurines. But the real quirk of this bar isn't the great atmosphere created by the pianist at the piano or the resident fortune-teller, but rather the very famous yet indescribable baths with their many marble fountains.

The Bar del Fico, with its trendy design, colorful walls, and vintage decor, is a warm, friendly place, definitely somewhere for the young and the hip. You'll like meeting the interesting people who go there, and maybe even striking up a conversation with a celebrity while sipping a cocktail in the cafe's little piazza.

For those who like feeling at home, the perfect place is Les Affiches. The atmosphere here is relaxed, and the easy-chic regulars enjoy being just the way they are. When you're inside the café, be sure to glance up at the ceiling... the decor is pretty alternative.

What is really fun is to keep going from one place to another. Whether you're a Roman or not, once inside this triangle, you'll want to (and will) lose all other addresses for the evening. Just let yourself be carried along by the warmth of the evening and the friendly Roman atmosphere.

BAR DEL FICO
Piazza del Fico, 26
Tel. + 39 06 68891373
www.bardelfico.com

JONATHAN'S ANGELS
Via della Fossa, 16
Tel. + 39 06 6893426

LES AFFICHES
Via di Santa Maria dell'Anima, 52
Tel. +39 06 64760715 / +39 320 6360430

Go shopping in your lingerie

There is a store in the bustling central neighborhood of Prati where your audaciousness and bargain hunting will be put to the test.

All you have to do is simply keep an eye out for the crazy promotions that are on offer in store from time to time. Then, hurry to get those dizzying heels, that super sexy dress, or the most original T-shirts for next to nothing.

Those who are familiar with the promotions of this label know that at Halloween, for example, they'll get a 50% discount just by coming

in fancy dress, or that during Bikini's Week, they'll be able to buy any article for 5 Euros just by coming into the shop – dressed only in their underwear!

So, get ready for lots of fun... and lots of unbeatable savings!

IRON G

Via Cola di Rienzo, 50

Tel. +39 06 3216798 / +39 393 4646436

Via del Gambero, 7/A

Tel. +39 06 45551480

iron@iron-g.com – www.iron-g.com

Take a cookery course in the temple of taste

Italian cuisine certainly needs no introduction; it is famous and loved the world over. It will be an endless source of inspiration for any woman looking to try her hand at its most renowned dishes. If you're looking for more than just a good cookbook or a few cooking programs on TV, there is a place in Rome where you can learn to make all of your favorite dishes

with a real Italian chef by your side. The Città del Gusto is a veritable culinary temple dedicated to taste. It offers cookery classes for amateurs who want to learn to cook in its well equipped kitchen-classrooms. Under the supervision of qualified chefs/professors, you will learn all the secrets of Italian cuisine.

After being assigned your workspace at the beginning of the lesson, you will study the recipes that you will be preparing and learn all about the typical ingredients.

Then comes the practical part of the lesson. This gives you the chance to practice alongside a chef and his or her assistants.

And then finally... you'll be able to sit down and enjoy the dishes you've prepared!

There are all sorts of courses, and except for a few set programs, they change continuously, using the fresh products of each season.

You can choose from different kinds of regional cooking too, whether Roman, Sicilian or Neapolitan, or learn to bake bread and pizza. There are courses on foreign cooking too (sushi, paella, etc.), or you can focus on first and second meat or fish courses only, or spoon desserts, or finger food...

There are also interesting themed lessons: cooking for a surprise party, a romantic dinner, or "cheap and chic" event. There are courses designed for singles – a great way to meet people and share your common interests.

Afraid of forgetting everything you've learned? Relax!

At the end of the course, you'll be given all of the recipes and instructions – and even your very own Gambero Rosso apron!

SCUOLA DEL GAMBERO ROSSO
CITTÀ DEL GUSTO
Via Enrico Fermi, 161
Tel. +39 06 551121
formazione@gamberorosso.it

Discover what the worst nightmare of every Roman girl is

It's Monday, your working day is almost over and you've already got one foot out the door. You're looking forward to that gym class and getting back into shape after the little excesses of the weekend. What could be better for overcoming your guilt about all the junk you ate, how much you drank and how late you stayed out than a good workout?

As you leave the gym, of course your make up is ruined and your hair is a disaster, but what does it matter, you feel great.

But suddenly a dark cloud gathers in the horizon. Remember that good-looking guy, a few years older than you, who lives on the fifth floor? The one who is always so fresh and impeccably dressed? The one who you

dream of going out on a date with one day? Well, there he is, suddenly out of nowhere, waiting in front of the lift with you. He looks you up and down.

An instant later you're in the lift together, and up you go for what seems like an eternity.

Nothing you can do now about the runny Rimmel under both eyes that makes you look like uncle Fester in person. Or your hair, which is all stuck to your face and makes you look like a cat just out of the rain... Truly terrifying. A real nightmare!

Know for sure
when it's noon in Rome

Do you know how Romans know it's midday? Go to Gianicolo Hill and you'll hear a cannon that fires blanks everyday at 12 on the dot.

This famous tradition was introduced in 1847 by Pope Pius IX so that all of the churches of Rome could be synchronized according to the precise official time.

Though initially the cannon was fired from the Castel Sant'Angelo, in 1903 it was moved to Monte Mario. On 24 January 1904 the cannon was transferred to Gianicolo, where it remains today. During WWII the tradition was suspended, but was resumed again in 1959.

Once you are at Gianicolo, be sure to stop for a quiet aperitif at the **Baretto** on Via Garibaldi. This is the road that descends from Gianicolo Hill to Trastevere. The Baretto is nice both indoors and outdoors, immersed in green, and has a retro feel.

There are bistro chairs and tables, an old jukebox, and there are never the same paintings on the walls. In the evening, candles and soft lights create a really cool atmosphere!

IL BARETTO
Via Giuseppe Garibaldi, 28
Tel. + 39 06 5896055
Monday to Friday 6:00 pm to 2:00 am
Saturday and Sunday 8:00 am to 2:00 am

Make peace with the city

Romans are inexorably in love with their city and they all consider Rome as the most beautiful city in the world. Yet, just as in any love relationship, there might be a few quarrels now and then between Rome and its inhabitants.

At least once a week all Romans say they wished they lived somewhere else. They'd love to just run away and leave the city. Of course, there's nothing fun about being in Rome on the day of a subway strike or during torrential rain. There are also the many events in the Capital that Romans are forced to put up with (demonstrations, cultural events, the elections of Popes and presidents, official State visits...).

As a result, the city can become a place of chaos and a source of great stress for all of its inhabitants!

One might truly wonder how the city can be loved so much, despite it all. Indeed, it is not only because it is the Eternal City and its beauty is incomparable. Perhaps it is also because, just like a beautiful woman with whom we are in love, Rome always manages to make peace with its inhabitants.

There are moments the city offers, when you least expect them, that will make you forget everything else. All is forgiven.

One of Rome's sunsets is enough to make peace with the city. Though there are many places to go and admire them, perhaps the most beautiful sunsets are the ones you just happen to see by chance.

The best times are definitely in spring and summer, after heavy rain or a dry windy day, when the sky is clear and the colors are extraordinary.

All you have to do is be on the lungotevere that runs near the historical center (the Mausoleo di Augusto, Piazza del Popolo or

Ponte Umberto I). Or the bypass from the Foro Italico (right after Via Salaria), or even the Via Cristoforo Colombo, heading towards Ostia. Then, suddenly, we see a thousand burning nuances as the sun slowly descends over the city...

You'll definitely want to take a photo of this incredible spectacle with your smartphone and then post it on Facebook.

It will be the right moment to reconcile yourself with a city that is impossible not to love.

Learn the seven superstitions of Roman etiquette: solutions

1. There cannot be thirteen dinner guests at the table, so it is better to opt for finger food or a buffet.

   Why: Thirteen around the table would bring misfortune since at the Last Supper the thirteenth person was Jesus Christ, who was crucified. According to popular belief, the thirteenth guest will have bad luck or will die before the end of the year! We have never heard of any other famous precedents though...

2. Do not place pieces of cutlery on top of one another to form a cross.

   Why: The cross formed by the cutlery recalls the death of Christ, therefore it is advisable to avoid it.

3. Do not refold your napkin the way you found it when you sat down to dinner.

   Why: This means that you have not enjoyed the meal and therefore this is not a very polite thing to do.

4. Never play cards or any other game when the table is set and covered with a tablecloth.

   Why: This recalls the scene of the Roman soldiers who played dice for Christ's garments.

5. When a guest asks you to pass the salt, put the shaker near the person but let the guest pick it up himself.

   Why: No one really knows why, but it's always better not to push your luck!

6. At the end of a dinner, as you leave your host's house, do not put your seat back under the table.

   Why: This means that you will never come back to that house again, so here again it is better not to offend your host.

7. When you pour any drink into another guest's glass, whether wine or water, always make sure to fill the glass generously.

   Why: According to a popular saying, a glass should be full enough so that the devil cannot dance in the empty space. However, more likely this is only a way of asking the host not to be too parsimonious with the wine. The important thing is not to go overboard and run the risk of transforming this gesture into something not particularly chic.